Lyndsay Green is a pioneering sociologist and researcher who has spent her career helping people use communications technologies for learning. Motivated by her aging parents and family, she has now turned her research skills and knowledge of new technologies to find out what the baby-boom generation should be doing to ensure its members have a successful old age. Green is a highly sought-after speaker and moderator at national and international organizations. The American textbook *Computers and Information Systems* calls Green an "information agent of the future."

Books of Merit

Praise for *You Could Live a Long Time*

"If you, like me, are finally becoming aware of your mortality and are beginning to wonder if the final third of your life will either be a living hell or a fascinating road to the hereafter, then you'll love the insights this perceptive 'pollster' has garnered from her 40 remarkably wise elders mixed in with solid social science and lots of her own common sense."

— MICHAEL ADAMS,
author of *Fire and Ice: The United States, Canada and the Myth of Converging Values* and president of Environics

"The road to Crowd Invisible doesn't have to be littered with loneliness and boredom, as you will learn in Lyndsay's book. Discover how others have found the secret to fun and fulfillment. The surprise is that it is *not* all about money."

— VICKI GABEREAU

"Throughout her career, Lyndsay Green has anticipated the next trend in communications and has been right there, imparting expertise and vision, most often to organizations which contribute enormously to the 'human capital' of our whole democracy. Now she's doing it again by tackling the greying of the boomers."

— MARILOU MCPHEDRAN,
Principal, Global College, The University of Winnipeg

You Could Live a Long Time: Are You Ready?

Lyndsay Green

THOMAS ALLEN PUBLISHERS
TORONTO

Library and Archives Canada Cataloguing in Publication

Green, Lyndsay
    You could live a long time : are you ready? / Lyndsay Green.

Includes bibliographical references.

ISBN 978-0-88762-527-5

1. Aging—Psychological aspects. 2. Baby boom generation—Life skills guides.
3. Older people—Life skills guides. 4. Old age—Social aspects. I. Title.

BF724.55.A35G74   2010   155.67   C2009-907222-X

Editor: Katherine Ashenburg
Cover design: Sputnik Design Partners Inc.
Cover image: Jupiter Images

Published by Thomas Allen Publishers,
a division of Thomas Allen & Son Limited,
145 Front Street East, Suite 209,
Toronto, Ontario M5A 1E3 Canada

www.thomas-allen.com

The publisher gratefully acknowledges the support of the Ontario Arts
Council for its publishing program.

We acknowledge the support of the Canada Council for the Arts, which last
year invested $20.1 million in writing and publishing throughout Canada.

We acknowledge the Government of Ontario through the Ontario Media
Development Corporation's Ontario Book Initiative.

We acknowledge the financial support of the Government of Canada
through the Book Publishing Industry Development Program (BPIDP)
for our publishing activities.

10 11 12 13 14 5 4 3 2 1

Printed and bound in Canada

*This book is dedicated to my own role models—
my parents Joan and Stuart Green, my aunts
Jean MacLachan and Joy Anderson, my uncle
Cecil Anderson, and my mother- and father-
in-law Joan and Bill Intven.*

Contents

Acknowledgments

My heartfelt thanks goes to the forty elders who were extraordinarily generous in sharing the experiences and advice of a lifetime. They are Warren Allmand, Sydney Bacon, Bob Breadon, Beth Breadon, Doris Connell, Maurice Cowper-Smith, Marion Dewar, Edra Ferguson, Dorothy Fetterly, Madelaine Field, Dick Goldbloom, Ruth Goldbloom, Alan Grant, Phyllis Grosskurth, Andrew Hazeland, Jane Heffelfinger, Margarite Hunt, Ida Ker, Marjorie Koller, Muriel Laing, Laurier LaPierre, Mary Large, Flora MacDonald, Helen MacLean, Jenny Mansfield, Margaret McBurney, Bob McMullen, John Meisel, Maureen Molaro, Pat Morrow, Wanda O'Hagan, Gertrude Robinson, Blair Seaborn, George Shaw, Anna Sirek, Ricardo Smith, Sadie Stern, Claire Taylor, Jim Westcott and Nancy Westcott. A special thanks goes to all those who helped me identify these terrific role models, including Barb Emery, Marie Morgan, Coleen

Quinn, Andrea Shaw, Janice Skinner, Jeannie Thomas and Gail Valaskakis. I am extremely grateful to the following people who reviewed the manuscript and greatly improved the book with their knowledge and insights: Suzie Cunningham, Susannah Dalfen, Barb Emery, Vince Gilpin, Gerri Grant, Ann Kirkland, Biff Matthews, Marcia McClung, Maureen McEvoy, Elizabeth Moody, Sean Moore, Susan Oldfield, Judy Parker, Dr. Guy Proulx, Suzanne Robinson, Ben Singer, Judy Steed and Lillian Zimmerman. I received valuable ideas for publishing, marketing and distributing the book from many people, including Catherine Allman, Sara Angel, Anne Carlyle, Janine Cocker, Bronwyn Drainie, Pamela Earle, Ross Mayot, Marilou McPhedran, Helen Walsh and Grace Westcott. My publisher, Patrick Crean, and editor, Katherine Ashenburg, have blessed this book with their expertise and enthusiasm. And, it is the unstinted love and support of my husband, Hank, and daughters, Lauren and Andrea, that makes all things possible.

You Could Live a Long Time: Are You Ready?

Background

I HAVE sometimes thought about what I might do if I found out that I had only a few weeks to live. One of those times was after the sudden and untimely death of a dear friend. But I am beginning to realize that there is a much tougher and probably more likely scenario. I might have a long life. Before jazz musician and composer Eubie Blake died at the age of 96, he mused, "If I'd known I was going to live this long, I would have taken better care of myself." Blake died over a quarter of a century ago, so his surprise was quite plausible. But I won't be able to make the same claim. I know that the average life expectancy is rising dramatically and I fit the longevity profile. I'm already 60 years old; I have no major health issues; and I come from long-living stock. So, barring a killer disease or an accident, I am likely to become old—maybe even very old. Around me I see some people living out their elder years with great satisfaction, but many others would have wished for a shorter life sentence. What makes the difference? Is there something I could be doing now to make it more likely that I live well—right to the end?

To answer these questions I decided I needed some guides—people who are now in the country of the aged and are mastering the landscape. My goal was to gather the accumulated wisdom from these successful seniors and use their insights to compile a guide to what lies ahead. I would use their tips to prepare for the future. To find the guides, I canvassed friends and acquaintances and asked them to recommend people over the age of 75 who were their role models. When I asked people for suggestions, my criterion was simple. "Who do you want to be when you grow up?" Some people could not name a single older person they felt was a role model. Some had been traumatized by experiences with elderly relatives or friends, and could only come up with negative examples. But finding the role models didn't take long, and with input from hundreds of people, I selected forty men and women between the ages of 75 and 100 who were living in seven cities from one end of Canada to the other.

For the advice to be broadly applicable, I looked for people from a range of backgrounds with a variety of occupations, educational and income levels. I deliberately avoided the rich, the famous and the exceptional, whose examples might leave me breathless with awe, but despondent over my own limitations. I wanted to talk with people who were living lives to which I could relate. The forty elders I interviewed include nurses, teachers, professors, lawyers, doctors, engineers and business people, and nearly a quarter had no post-secondary degree. As Richard told me proudly, "I graduated from UHK (University of Hard Knocks)." The real names of the elders are listed in the acknowledgments to this book, but I promised to change their names and disguise their identities in the body of the book. Because our discussions were about life's most intimate details, I made this commitment to allow people to speak as candidly as possible. My goal was to combine the role models' wisdom with a wide range of reading on the subject, to identify the practical decisions and techniques that would let me make use of their advice right away. I was feeling the wind of age on my back and I wanted to get moving.

In the following pages I examine the anxieties about aging that led me to pursue this research, and outline my own misconceptions about growing old. What the elders taught me turned my thinking on its head. Their most important lessons are almost all paradoxical: they run counter to our society's obsession with staying forever young, and to my own assumption that I must fight aging at all costs. Instead, aging well depends on an acceptance, sometimes even an embrace, of the aging process. The role models have become my inspiration. I would be happy to live the final stretch with their courage, integrity and grace—not to mention their sheer delight at still being alive. To be honest, I was tempted to skip writing this book, and concentrate on putting their advice into practice as fast as I could. It was guilt that made me change my mind. This book is in your hands because a friend, who was watching me making life changes based on the elders' advice, admonished me for my selfishness: "You're implementing and not sharing." So here it is— I'm passing along everything I've learned. You can thank my friend Suzanne.

My Introduction to Elderland

I T WAS during my third visit to my aunt's long-term-care facility that I realized I'd never survive old age unless I started preparing. I shared my anxiety at the time with a friend who replied, "What do we need to do? We're only in our fifties." At this point I hadn't progressed past fear, and had no strategies, so I grasped at the one quality I thought was going to save my aunt. "We're going to have to become charming, utterly charming." She, being my friend, replied, "But you're already very charming." My retort was ominous—and would prove to be accurate. "Not nearly charming enough."

My first visit with Aunt Jean at Garden Village, or Tuscan Sunset (the name is unimportant), was the day I helped her move in. This event rang no alarm bells. On the contrary, everything went beautifully. At 86 years of age, Jean had decided it was no longer safe for her to be living alone in her apartment. Although she was still sharp as a tack, with a memory better than mine, her walking had deteriorated and she'd started to fall. One reason that first day went so well was because Jean had used her charm to enlist my help and that of our friend Mary Lou. While Jean and I completed the admissions paperwork in the office, Mary Lou moved Jean's belongings into her new room. She took great pains to arrange Jean's new living space as a scaled-down version of the apartment she'd just left, complete with afghan-covered comfy chair and the highlights of her career framed on the wall. When Jean walked into her new room she couldn't have been happier; she felt right at home.

Even the second visit didn't make me nervous, focused as we were on understanding all the procedures and learning where the services were located. But by the third visit, both Jean and I were starting to get the picture that her life had changed dramatically, and not for the better. Because of the mental and physical limitations of her tablemates, Jean was unable to carry on intelligible conversations at mealtimes, let alone have the stimulating discussions she enjoyed. The recreational options, geared as they were to the capacity and interests of the majority of the residents, were stultifyingly boring. And, to fit the nursing schedules, Jean had to be woken at 6 a.m.

every morning so the nurse could put pressure bandages on her legs. The future looked grim. My aunt had always run her own show. She was a career woman who had never married and was used to being the sole woman in management in her company. As one of the care facility staff put it, "Jean, you don't belong here." But this was the path she had chosen and she was determined to live this last phase of her life with the grace, dignity and good humour that were her trademarks.

As the months went by, I realized I had been quite prescient in identifying my aunt's charm as her saving grace. For my aunt survived, even thrived, by making deep connections with pretty well everyone she encountered in her new home. Many of her care workers were new arrivals to Canada and Jean became their teacher—helping them understand cultural peculiarities, fill out government forms and assist with their children's homework. She became best friends with the senior staff, who turned to her for wisdom, political insights and recipes. She became a confidante to the 26-year-old graduate student who was working part-time as the residence administrator to earn money for his studies. As he told me, he could talk to Jean about anything; she was his dearest friend.

The day Jean suffered a stroke the staff knew from experience that she was unlikely to return from the hospital. When the attendants took her by stretcher out of the building for transfer to the ambulance, she was surrounded by staff members who came to kiss her goodbye. The attendants said that in all their years of transferring elderly patients from retirement homes, they had never seen such a display of affection. Jean died in hospital a few weeks later of complications from the stroke. She was almost 90 and had lived in the seniors' home for three years. Jean had been quick to size up her situation in the home and early on decided to capitalize on its best asset: the lively and caring staff. Although she had been forced to give up her valued independence, she swapped it for a life of loving interdependence, and I think she would have said that, in the end, it was a fair trade.

If my only experience in the land of the elderly had been with my aunt I might have simply shelved the lesson as a note to self: "Attend charm school before it's too late." But, as it turned out, I was only at the first staging point of a long journey into Elderland, a journey that would turn my assumptions about aging inside out and drive home my early premonition that I'd better start preparing immediately for what lay ahead. After my aunt Jean died, her sister, my aunt Joy, who was nearly 80 at the time, became ill with a rare and inoperable form of cancer. I spent hours with her in the palliative care ward of a seniors' health centre. It turned out that Joy had lucked into spending the final months of her life in one of the most progressive long-term-care facilities in the country. As I spent time with her and her caregivers, I had a chance to see examples of the leading thinking in eldercare, where art and music are an integral part of the environment, and the institution has its own art curator. Several times when I was visiting Joy in her room, a musician came around to play guitar and sing to the patients; another time, a volunteer dropped in with a gift—a red rose. If Joy had been in better health she would have been able to participate in the many hands-on creative arts programs that the staff see as integral to hope and healing. But what really allowed Joy to die with dignity was the relationship she forged with a young woman student rabbi who spent hours sitting by her bedside. It was her discussions about life and loss, the body and the spirit, birth and death, that brought Joy a sense of blessed peace when she breathed her last.

All this experience would pale in comparison with my current voyage, the one I am taking with my parents. For the past several years my brothers and I have been trying to support their failing physical and mental health. My parents, both in their early eighties, were determined to remain in their home of thirty-five years. Although they recognized that living in their house was increasingly unsafe for them, they resisted their children's efforts to move them to a more manageable place. They told us they had decided to wait for "an accident" that would force a move. That accident came two years ago, when my mother fell out of bed and fractured her collarbone. She was taken to the emergency ward and never returned home. After a few weeks in hospital, she was sent to the one long-term-care facility that had an available bed. For the next few months my father took lengthy bus trips to visit her daily, but became unable to cope on his own in the house. He moved to a retirement residence that was close to my mother's facility and the house was sold. Since then, my mother's changing care needs have placed her in six different locations, including hospitals, retirement homes and long-term-care facilities. My father followed her around to try to stay close, sometimes living with her in the same facility, and sometimes in another location within walking distance. At this point, they are together, living on different floors of an excellent long-term-care facility, and we all hope there will be no more moves.

The most hard-hitting lesson from my parents' experience is that by waiting for an accident, they gave up control of their future. Before my mother had her injury, they had many options for highly desirable accommodation. By waiting until it was too late, she was forced to take an available bed in a most depressing and unsatisfactory facility, and it took all the family's resources and two years of effort to get the two of them where they are now. It became the ultimate irony: my mother did not want to leave her home because she did not want any more moves. As a result, she had to endure six moves in two years.

Confronting My Misconceptions

A S I SPENT hour upon hour in the institutions where we care for our elderly, it gradually dawned on me that I had it all wrong. I had been making some grave errors in my thinking about old age and about my own future.

Misconception #1: My preoccupation should be figuring out how to live longer.

The obvious goal seems to be to live as long a life as possible. Our average life expectancy is increasing, and surely this is an absolute good, both for me and everyone else. Isn't longevity just another one of those indices of prosperity where higher is better? In the abstract this makes sense, but I now see the problem. We're extending the end of our life, not the beginning.[1] My father nailed the issue one day when we were visiting my mother in the long-term-care facility where she lived. As we watched the rows of elderly people waiting to be toileted and fed, he turned to me and said, "We're not living longer, we're dying longer." My father was 85 years old at the time, and I realized that we had set out to find the fountain of youth, but ended up with the fountain of age. So I am now worrying about just how old I might get. My grandmother was nearly 92 when she died and you know about the rest of my immediate family's longevity. I posed the question to a life-expectancy calculator I found at the website www.livingto100.com. The prediction: I am going to live to 104. Instead of worrying that I might not live long enough, my anxiety is now around living too long.

Misconception #2: I will die a "good death," which means living a long life in which I am vigorously firing on all cylinders, and then suddenly flame out, preferably in my sleep.

A long life wouldn't necessarily be bad news if only I hadn't been forced to re-examine my assumption that I would live a vigorous life that ended abruptly in a "good death." I found out that my dream of being a *well elder* and then suddenly moving directly to the exit door is so common it even has a name. Experts on aging label this goal *compressing morbidity*, which is perfectly captured by the carriage in Oliver Wendell Holmes's poem "The Deacon's Masterpiece." The carriage is built so well that not a single part breaks down for a hundred years. Then it collapses *"all at once, and nothing first/Just as bubbles do when they burst."* But what were the odds of this happening to me? I needed to find a life expectancy calculator that understood the difference between *just breathing* and *having a life* and found one at www.bluezones.com. Their calculation predicts that I'll live to 98, but I'll only be healthy until age 90. This unsettling assessment seemed more in keeping with my own observations.[2] Yes, there are some people who do live fully and then die abruptly, but I'd better not count on being one of them.

Misconception #3: My old self would be just like my young self, only greyer and saggier.

Spending copious amounts of time in the company of the elderly and their families has led me to rethink my assumption that I would age into someone who was the same, only older. Instead, it seems more likely that mental and physical changes will bring my senior self new struggles and different preoccupations, and I will need to cultivate new strengths and find new strategies. In the extreme case I might develop dementia, but even barring such a dramatic development, I would still be changed by the physical, mental, psychological and socio-cultural struggles that confront the elderly. I saw this with my own family and have heard similar stories from many other people. A trusting man becomes paranoid and suspects people of stealing his soap. A mathematical whiz is unable to make change at the store. A woman who never swore in her life sprinkles her conversation with vulgarities. A man who loved his independence is afraid to stay alone. It also seemed that some of the things I was putting off until I got older—my family genealogy, donating my collections, organizing my papers, adventure travel—might require skills I would no longer have. As I put on the lens of the seniors around me, I saw that life was different through their eyes. So I had to face the likelihood that I would not be the same person that I am today.

Misconception #4: Living the good life in my old age would be all about health and wealth.

The bulk of advice in self-help books on aging is about acquiring wealth and staying healthy, but, while health and wealth are important, I became convinced they wouldn't be enough to guarantee me a good life in those final years. First, I won't be healthy. If I live to a ripe old age, it is inevitable that I will have health problems. After all, those of us in our late fifties and early sixties are already complaining about arthritis, high blood pressure, underactive thyroids, back problems, heart disease, diabetes, and problems seeing and hearing. And many of us have battled cancer and other life-threatening diseases and are living with the aftermath. Increasingly, medical science can fix things, but both the treatments and the recovery can be pretty onerous. Aunt Jean had quadruple bypass heart surgery at age 80 and it gave her nearly another decade of life. But the months of rehabilitation after the operation were pretty grim, and the incision on her leg, where they had extracted blood vessels for the bypass, caused her problems to the end of her life. So, being old will mean accepting less than perfect health, and certainly some pain.

As for money, it was clear that having adequate financial resources would give me more options as I age. But it started to sink in that money alone will be insufficient for living well in Elderland. Many aspects of the support I will need, I won't be able to purchase. For example, I can hire people to be my caregivers (i.e., to care *for* me), but money alone won't guarantee that they will care *about* me. And, if my caregivers haven't the time to get to know me, and have limited knowledge of my personal history, they'll have a hard time interpreting my needs. Also, to benefit from my financial resources, I'll need to have trusted attentive advisers who will help me spend my money in ways that will enhance my well-being. As I wandered through Elderland, I began to understand that many of the people sitting alone and miserable in their rooms were not lacking financial assets. So I made a calculation of the cost of the daily effort, expertise and dedication that I will need to sustain a high quality of life when I'm old, and realized I'd need more than cash.

Misconception #5: The skill and talents that are working for me now will make me a successful senior.

Once I concluded that health and wealth weren't going to be enough to guarantee a successful stay in Elderland, I needed to figure out what strengths I should be working on. I began to suspect that the skills that have been so critical to my success to date weren't the ones I would need moving forward. For example, it looked as if my ability to complete tasks with a perfectionist's high standard of competence was not going to endure, even if it were desirable. And what about that stiff-upper-lip approach to challenges that emphasized stoicism, capability and keeping one's problems to oneself? And how far would independent problem-solving and strategic thinking take me? I had the feeling that the things that got me here weren't going to get me there. And maybe these skills would no longer be part of my senior self anyway. I realized that I had better start now to develop what I was going to need—beginning with Aunt Jean's famous charm.

Having worked through my preconceptions, I had to face the following realities: I might live a long life; I couldn't count on a quick, easy exit; old age might change me in unpredictable ways; health and wealth would not be sufficient; moving forward was going to require as yet undefined resources. So this became my mission, to find out what qualities and assets I would need to navigate the terrain in Elderland, and figure out how to acquire them.

What I discovered was that a series of paradoxes are embedded in many aspects of life in Elderland, and much of the advice contained in these paradoxes runs counter to the attitudes about aging that confront us daily. I now understand that to age successfully, instead of fighting to stay young, we should embrace aging. Instead of focusing exclusively on augmenting our RRSPs, we should be cultivating what will become the most valuable part of our retirement plan: our emotional circle of friends and families, and partners. To stay attractive to others, we need to spend more time focusing on our inner selves, and less time having facelifts and hair implants. To keep our physical agility, we have to stop pushing our bodies and pretending to be young. If we want to retain our independence as we age, we must learn to accept help.

These paradoxes of aging, along with many more, are explored in the following sections that look at all aspects of our aging selves: our emotional circle, our self, our civic engagement, our work, our home, our body, our brain, our finances, our legacy, and our collective future. The wisdom of the elders, coupled with the techniques unearthed in my research, provide concrete ways to grapple with what lies ahead.

Our Emotional Circle

The most valuable part of your Retirement Savings Plan is your emotional circle, and it can't be bought.

AFTER what I learned from the elders, I'm building up my RECP (Retirement Emotional Circle Plan), and giving it as much weight as my RRSP (Registered Retirement Savings Plan). I will need to cultivate the richest possible social network, one that includes friends as well as family, because I will need to draw upon these resources as I age. On a practical level, I'll need my network for assistance with daily living. But the emotional support will be even more important. As the grandmother says to her grandson in Alistair MacLeod's novel *No Great Mischief*, "We're all better when we're loved." And, if I have the support of friends and family in my senior years there's a good chance that I'll be happier and healthier—both mentally and physically. Researchers aren't certain why, but they're finding a strong link between the health, well-being and quality of life of older people, and the strength and quality of their social relationships and community engagement. One speculation is that hanging out with other people promotes healthy behaviour and reduces stress levels.[1] Even if I'm in poor health, I'll be less likely to suffer from depression if I have frequent contact with friends.[2] There is also some startling research that loneliness can actually increase the risk of Alzheimer's.[3] There is even speculation that those famously healthy Mediterranean people may be healthy, not because of their diet, but because they enjoy high levels of social interaction, and deep and sustaining emotional networks.[4]

The elders advise us to strengthen our bonds with the three significant components of our emotional circle—our friends, our partner and our family, and their advice illuminates the inherent paradox.

Now, when you're too busy for your friends, is the time you should be working to keep them and to make new ones.

Now is the time to make and keep good friends because the older we get, the more important they will become. Friends will laugh with us, give us a hand, allow us to help them in return, participate with us in life's remaining adventures and share our memories. If we nurture our friendships over the years, we will have a storehouse of intimacy and caring to draw on as we age.

It will be particularly important for us boomers to focus on friends because our family networks are smaller and weaker than those of our parents. Our generation had children late, we have divorced and remarried more frequently, we raised more children in single-parent households, had smaller families, and a large number of us never married. So, whereas today most seniors get their help with daily chores from their relatives,[5] boomers shouldn't count on being able to repeat this pattern. Urban planner Gerald Hodge takes this factor into account in his recommendations for designing "Senior-Smart" communities. "Probably the most hopeful outcome for seniors of extended family structures will be stronger bonds with their peers," he says. "This will be especially important to the one-third or more who live alone."[6]

Carol's active social life gives me an insight into the importance of friends in later life. "I'm 85 and some of my friends are the same age as me, and some are younger. It's quite a big group; there are about a dozen of us. I took Betty to the hairdresser's to get a permanent on Sunday. Several of us are playing bridge tomorrow. And I'm having breakfast with other friends on Thursday. We go to movies regularly, and we all go out to breakfast four to five times a year to celebrate birthdays. Everyone is very kind and anxious to do something for somebody else. Your children are a comfort to you. They phone you once a week. But it's your friends you need."

Carol's example notwithstanding, it's worrisome to note that about one out of every ten people over 65 say they have no friends.[7] And more than four out of five seniors aged 75 and over have not met any new people in the last month whom they intend to befriend.[8] As boomers, one might think we're in a better position than older people to make and keep friends. We're still in the workforce and many of us are engaged in the community through our children. But it's easy to neglect our friends for these same reasons. Several of the elders told me this happened to them. "One thing I regret is that, because I was so busy, I lost a lot of close friendships," Peter says. "Time would go by and then I'd realize we hadn't seen each other for years. Maintaining friendships takes time. I'm making new contacts all the time but it's tough to keep the old ones, especially with people moving all over the place." Stan had the same problem. He is 80 now and says that if he were able to turn back the clock and be 50 again he would focus more on friendships. "I should have worked harder at cultivating good friends and keeping them. I've been kind of self-centred, and my old friends have gradually dropped off."

It's easy to confuse an acquaintance with a friendship. At work, for example, colleagues may look like friends, and the difference may only become apparent when we leave our job. As William explains, "People will tell you that they'll keep in touch. But it doesn't happen. It can be especially difficult for people with big jobs who have been surrounded by 'yes' men and women. They think they are all-powerful, and popular—but then, all of a sudden, they have nothing. So you need to figure out who will still be there for you when you have nothing to offer but yourself. That's a friend."

Fred proposes this friendship test: "If you lose your mate, who will continue to see you?" Fred, now 81, was widowed ten years ago and never expected to be alone at this age. "It's terrible when you lose your mate. People treat you differently. When death enters into the family, a good number of the friends you used to see regularly drop away."

Here are some more friendship tests offered by the elders. Norah asks, "If you are living alone, who will take you in for twenty-four hours after you've had a cataract operation like my friend did for me?" Or, in the case of Betty, "What friend would help provide the several weeks of care I needed after I broke my pelvis?"

But even as we nurture our old friendships, we'll need to keep making new friends. There is a very good reason for this, as Steve points out plainly: "You need to keep meeting new people because the old ones keep dying." When I was interviewing the elders it was not uncommon for them to have recently lost a loved one. Doreen at 90 years of age was mourning the loss of a dear friend who had died a few weeks before we spoke. "We played golf, tennis and bridge, and we were constantly together. I saw her more than anybody." Carol reminded me that death isn't the only way we will lose our friendships. "My close friend got Alzheimer's. I miss her companionship so much. We have been friends since we were three years old."

One of the things the elders had in common was a plethora of "young" friends. At 83 years of age, Dan makes a point of staying in touch with younger people. "My closest friends are my age, but it is helpful, stimulating and enjoyable to also have my friends who are twenty years younger. These people in their fifties and sixties help me stay younger and I get to hear what they're thinking. It's rather depressing being only among older people, especially as you begin to lose them." At age 90, Betty is passionate about spending time with people much younger—especially her grandchildren and their friends. "I get a lot of inner happiness when I see young people and I'm always learning something current."

Understanding the need for friendships is one thing, but making and keeping friends will take a deliberate effort. The elders urge us to keep in touch with our old friends, and suggest we participate in group activities in order to expand our circle and make new friends.

Keep in Touch

Even if we move far away from some of our oldest and dearest friends, there's no excuse for dropping them. The elders are proof of that. I was struck by the enormous effort many of them are making to stay in touch with people who are scattered far and wide. Henry is 84 and he and his close friend now live on opposite sides of the country, but on the first Tuesday of every month they talk for an hour on the phone. "We're very close. He is a wonderful friend, and his advice has probably helped me the most over the years. For example, he's the one who kept encouraging me to continue teaching as long as possible, and that's what has kept me mentally engaged, and in touch with young people." At 100 years of age Marie is frustrated that she hasn't been able to make new friends in her retirement residence. She's filling some of the gap by keeping up a correspondence with a friend in Florida. She says, "When I read her letters, it's as though we were never apart." Since Hugh's wife died two years ago, the support of his best friend has been more important than ever. They are both 98 now and live hundreds of kilometres apart, but their weekly phone calls have been enough to sustain a half century of friendship.

The challenges of aging make the phone a handy tool for staying close to those living nearby, too. At 91, Victoria still has a very active life, and she used to pick up her good friend Meredith in the car to join her on her outings. But Meredith's family has decided that Victoria's driving skills are no longer up to scratch. "Meredith always loved to come out with me. We had such fun. As far as I'm concerned, I'm still a pretty good driver, but her family is very protective of her. So now she's no longer allowed to go in the car with me. They explain it away by telling me she isn't well enough to go out, but I got the message. So I don't offer to drive her places anymore. Now she's pretty housebound, and I know she misses our little trips, so I make sure that we speak every two to three days on the telephone."

Gene Cohen, a professor of psychiatry who has been studying people over 60, promotes the idea of designating specific times for communications. He says that spontaneously getting in touch with friends and family as the mood strikes, the way I do now, won't be enough to maintain contact as we age. Like the elders and their weekly phone calls, he recommends following a regular contact schedule to establish a routine. He particularly favours written correspondence such as letters or emails because this helps to strengthen our brains at the same time that it reinforces our network of friends.[9]

The plethora of new communications technologies that are easy and convenient to use means that our generation has no excuse for not keeping in touch, but, apologies to Cohen, the example I'm going to use relies not at all on the written word. I recently phoned a dear friend that I've known for thirty years. We now live in different cities and I called her cellphone, assuming she was home. Instead, I reached her playing with her grandson in a park in another city where her son's family lives. She immediately took a photo of her adorable offspring playing on the swing and emailed it to me on the spot so that I could share the moment. Later that day she phoned me from an art gallery to talk excitedly about the exhibit she was viewing. I was able to find a video on the Web about the work she was looking at, and we were able to discuss the show, virtually. Most of the media we're now using so blithely to record and share our lives with friends and family didn't exist even a few years ago, so it's hard to imagine what will be there for us when we're old.

Merely having the tools, however, won't be enough, we'll still need to use them—and first, we'll need to learn how to use them. One excellent way to pick up the latest computer skills is to learn from the young, even the very young. Many years ago my friend was visiting from another city. As we sipped our tea she told me about her anxiety over the growing use of computers in her company. She was utterly intimidated by the new technology but knew she had no choice—she had to adapt to the digital world. As she put it: "If I could, I'd avoid it completely, but I still have a few years left before retirement." She recalls my response: "You sent me upstairs with your daughter so that we could work together on the computer. I watched her move the mouse and click away at all those icons as if it were indeed child's play. I decided right then and there that I was not going to be bettered by a 5-year-old. I look back on this as one of the more humiliating moments of my life—but it sure lit a fire under me!" Although this training session took place nearly two decades ago, the principle still applies.

Join Groups

Being part of a group is a great way to make and keep friends, and it looks as if the loners among us would be wise to find our inner joiner. The elders belong to a multitude of groups organized around a vast diversity of subjects: book discussions, bridge, fitness, the arts, sports, religion and volunteer activities, and, as Georgina's story illustrates, belonging to groups has brought them many benefits. "For many years, and up until my retirement," she told me, "I worked with my husband in a consulting company we owned. I decided to retire when I was in my fifties, and this was a few years ahead of my husband. I woke up day one of my retirement and it really sunk in— I had no work to go to. I was quite at a loss. My husband and I had worked very closely together, so we were really in each other's pockets. I had the immediate question of what I'd do that day. But then I also got thinking about the days and years ahead. What would I do if anything happened to him? I realized I needed to widen my circle—and fast. Then I found out that I was on the verge of [developing] osteoporosis and that gave me another incentive to get going. Now I'm really engaged. I go to 'Friends in Fitness' and they are indeed my friends as well as my fitness buddies. I also have a walking group that goes out every Tuesday in spring and fall. Several years ago I found a group of women that grew out of the Great Books reading program. They're mostly around my age and we meet once a month. Over the years, these discussions have been a kind of therapy for me. I recommend you get involved in activities like these to make sure you have a lot of people around you. All these women would really be there for me if I needed them."

Gene Cohen stresses the importance of group participation as we age. He says that successful retirement requires what he calls "a balanced social portfolio," one that includes group activities as well as private activities, with both a mix of energetic and quiet activities. In his book *The Mature Mind: The Positive Power of the Aging Brain*, Cohen explains that the duration of an activity is more important than the nature of the activity, with a regular book club meeting contributing more to well-being than one-shot activities. Transient or non-interpersonal activities just don't give us the same opportunities to make new friends. He gives the example of one of his study participants, an opera buff. He didn't make friends by attending the opera and it was only when he began hosting an opera video and dinner club at his home that his friendships formed.[10]

Susan is 84 and has been widowed for twenty-two years. When her husband died she stayed alone in their home on an acreage in northern Canada for fourteen years. Several years ago, at the urging of her son, she moved to the big city to be closer to him and his family. She found it difficult to replicate the strong social networks of her former home. But, by keeping in touch regularly with old friends by mail and phone, she was able to retain her sense of community. In particular, her friendship with her quilting group from home became a lifeline. "Even though I have moved far away, they still keep in touch with me. They send me their newsletters, and one member of the group has made me her pen pal. We talk on the phone every week, and she has even come to visit. The group was started by a wonderful bunch of friends about twenty years ago, and it's not about the quilting, it's about the friendship. Once you reach 60 you should join something. That way you'll meet people you can keep in touch with for the rest of your life, no matter where you go. I would feel quite alone without them. It has made all the difference."

At 84, Sylvia has found that her participation in non-profit organizations has allowed her to stay connected with much younger people. Over the years she has been active on volunteer boards, and has made many friends this way. "They are people with whom I have a lot in common and even after I have left the organizations, the friendships continue to this day. Because I've been blessed with these friends who are ten and fifteen years younger, I forget how old I am."

For many of the elders, sports activities are a favourite way to forge and maintain friendships. Jeanette started playing golf when she was in her forties and is still play-ing at 82. "I play nine holes now with my friends and I don't want to give it up because of the friendships." At age 90, it's Richard's golf buddy who is keeping him company now that his wife has died. "It gets lonely at times with nobody to have dinner with. One of my golfing friends just lost his wife too and we have dinner together twice a week." Carol took up curling after she retired at 61. "I'd suggest curling to anyone. The people are lovely. It's not a competitive thing. It's just a vehicle for friendship." At 75, Peter is still playing hockey as much for the camaraderie as the exercise. "When I first started playing old-timer hockey I thought I'd probably play until I was 60, but I'm still at it. The other players are amazed, but I'd miss the friendship if I quit. I guess they'll have to carry me off." Virginia took up golf at 55 after being told, "Learn how to play golf and bridge and you'll always have friends when you're old."

In addition to meeting with people in the flesh, older people are finding friends and reducing loneliness on social networking sites like Facebook and MySpace. Paula Rice, at 73 years of age, spends fourteen hours a day on Eons.com, which calls itself an online community for spirited boomers. After a heart attack, Rice became housebound, and often a day goes by without her seeing another person. Her two marriages ended in divorce and her four children are scattered in other parts of the country. She says, "I was dying of boredom. Eons, all by its lonesome, gave me a reason to keep on going."[11] These friendships formed online may not have the weight of physical presence, but they still provide some of the benefits of an emotional circle.

There are groups for every interest and level of commitment, but not everyone takes to organized activity. If you fall into that category, simply meet the same people regularly for coffee—and you've got your group.

Become the Kind of Person You Would Want to Befriend

Keeping old friends and making new ones may require some brushing up of our interpersonal skills. I found it delightful to spend time with the elders because they had wit, humour and personal charm—but it was more than that. They have what we're increasingly calling emotional intelligence.[12] Here are their collective tips for dealing with people.

- Treat other people with mutual respect and acceptance.
- Never try to change the other person.
- Try not to be judgmental. Take people for who they are.
- Be ready to listen.
- Do not give advice unless it is asked for. If people want advice, they will ask for it.
- Behave with basic human kindness.
- Tell people you appreciate them when you get a chance.
- Be interested in other people. People who are secure and less self-centred age more easily.
- Don't take things personally or perceive slights where none are intended. Give people the benefit of the doubt.

- Make people smile, and even better—make them laugh!

All this is probably easier to do if we can remember to walk in the other person's shoes. Christine quoted Margaret Laurence's wise words on this subject. "I do not claim to pass on any secret of life, for there is none, or any wisdom except the passionate plea of caring . . . Try to feel, in your heart's core, the reality of others. This is the most painful thing in the world, probably, and the most necessary."[13] I think this ability was at the root of Aunt Jean's charm, and probably accounted for her success in forming relationships with most everyone she met. If I'm able to put this good advice into action, I'll probably not lack for company.

The elders gave me practical tips for being good company. Virginia says I must make an effort to stay current. "Keep up to date on everything you can—politics, art, books, movies. I read every day of my life." Gordon points out that I could combine staying current with exercise if I were to follow his example. He takes a daily walk to a downtown-hotel reading room where he scans all the international press, including *The New Yorker*, *Harper's*, and *The New York Review of Books*.

Malcolm reminded me that people aren't fun to be with if they stop gaining new experiences and are content to live in the past. "You must live in the present. There is nothing more boring than people going on about past successes." This same habit irritated psychoanalyst Carl Jung, who wrote, "Who does not know those touching old gentlemen who must always warm up the dish of their student days, who can fan the flame of life only by reminiscences of their heroic youth, but who, for the rest, are stuck in a hopelessly wooden Philistinism?... [T]hey are not neurotic, but only boring and stereotyped."[14]

The challenge in being a good conversationalist seems surprisingly unchanged. According to the seventeenth-century French author La Rochefoucauld, "One of the reasons why so few people are to be found who seem sensible and pleasant in conversation is that almost everybody is thinking about what he wants to say himself rather than about answering clearly what is being said to him."[15] That strikes a chord in modern as well as seventeenth-century ears. La Rochefoucauld's observation is found in *Conversation: A History of a Declining Art*, by Stephen Miller, which is a terrific resource for thinking about the meaning and importance of good conversation. The book includes many tips from centuries ago that remain relevant today.

Don't Go to Seed

While we need to accept aging gracefully, we will be more attractive if we don't let ourselves go to seed. When I asked Aunt Jean what I should be doing to prepare for my senior years, she said, "You'll need to learn to put on your face." She meant this advice in both its literal and abstract sense. She was encouraging me to learn how to apply makeup to enhance my physical attributes. She was also saying that I'll need to make an effort to be my best self when engaging with the world. She followed this advice herself without fail. She started every day in her retirement home by carefully applying her makeup with an expertise and a lightness of touch that was truly admirable. No smudged lipstick and bright blue eyeshadow for her. To her mind, this sent people the message that she respected them enough to want to look good for them. And she did the same thing with her mind. She prepared for my visits by informing herself about current affairs and the latest world events, and compiled a mental list of topics for us to discuss. She wanted to make each visit as engaging and stimulating as possible—for both of us. She seemed to make this same effort putting her best face forward—for everyone she met.

I was able to appreciate Aunt Jean's point about the need to rise to the occasion, but found myself resisting her advice on my appearance. I'm not much of a fashionista, and when it comes to makeup, I can't muster much more than lipstick. But after meeting the elders, I have reluctantly come around to Aunt Jean's point of view. When it comes to our aging selves, I have a new respect for the importance of externalities. Both the elderly men and the women I interviewed looked terrific, and their appearance was part of an overall engaging package—a creative and energetic presentation of self. They seemed to be making the effort to be their best selves, not merely because it felt good to look good, but as proof that they were still fully alive.

Looking as good as possible also attracts other people, as the Anglo-American writer Iris Origo noted in her autobiography, *Images and Shadows*. She took her two small daughters, who lived in Italy, on regular visits to her American grandmother, who was then in her eighties and nineties. Part of the reason the little girls adored their great-grandmother, she writes, was that she always looked and smelled so delicious. I am also reminded of my artistic friend, Agnes, who is always beautifully turned out and is great fun to be with. Now in her late seventies, she is the treasured travelling companion of an old friend who foots the bill because he enjoys her company. "I always dreamed of being able to see these exotic places," she says, "but, on my small pension, I could never have done it without Bill's help."

The 100-year-old Marie provides a good example of what we're talking about. When I visited her in the long-term-care home where she lived, I found her reclining on her hospital bed wearing an elegant caftan with her hair wrapped in a stylish turban. She would have been perfectly attired for entertaining royalty. She told me she was anxious to go home because she'd found it hard to make any good friends at the facility. She felt those around her were not good company because they had given up on themselves: "The people I've met here just don't make an effort." Marie says that part of looking good is not advertising your age. "Here's my advice to you. Don't tell people your age. They never get over it!" She was right. All the time I was talking with this glamorous, witty woman, I kept thinking to myself, "How is it possible that this woman is 100 years old?" She was correct in assuming I wouldn't be able to get over it, and my obsessing over her age gave it an importance it didn't deserve.

For some of the men amongst the elders, looking one's best means wearing a tie. At 98, Hugh always wears one, and Steve, at age 78, told me that he is resolved to wear one more often. He has been studying the older men he meets and concluded that the ones who look good are the ones who dress well. For Virginia, at 85, it's makeup. "I look and feel better with my face made up. If you do it first thing, it will last all day." When she was younger, her doctor told her, "Always make your face up, even if you don't feel well some days, and keep that up all your life." She also told me to watch my weight and take care of my skin. Several of the women advised me not to let my hair go white. Louise has her hair expertly dyed a vivacious henna colour and says, "My hairdresser has taken ten years off my age." However, more invasive forms of "putting on your face" were viewed as unnecessary. Peter's friend had just had a hair transplant. "His scalp was covered with horrible scabs," he says. "Why would you put yourself through that?"

But the way I talk about myself will be more important than the way I look. What Aunt Jean called "putting on my face" will also mean rising above the temptation to recite my medical ailments and list my daily travails to every passerby who makes the mistake of asking, "How are you?" As Betty says, "Nobody wants you around if you're gloom and doom." When all is said and done, a pleasant demeanour is still the best appearance enhancer. As Trudy says, "Go out and smile."

What the elders are telling me is that I shouldn't *let myself go to seed*, as the expression goes. In this context, the saying seems particularly apt. Just as a plant goes to seed after it flowers and is preparing to die, if I stop making an effort, it means I'm preparing for the end. At least, that is the message I'll be sending.

If you have a life partner, you need to figure out whether s/he is a partner for life.

If you have a partner, you'd better figure out whether he or she is the right one for the next inning. This is the advice from the elders, who span the spectrum themselves in terms of marital status, including the widowed, the single, the divorced, those who are still in their first marriage and those who have remarried. Several of those who have been widowed have found new partners, and some of the elders are in committed relationships but have not married. Their stories emphasize the critical role my partner will play in my senior years.

Marjorie learned the value of having the right partner when she saw what happened to her parents. "My father developed Alzheimer's when he was 69. He died at age 90, so he was essentially 'out of it' for twenty-one years. For the first eleven years of his illness, he lived at home with my mother. Then he moved to a long-term-care facility, and, after that, to a hospital. My mother visited him nearly every day. Watching her devotion made me appreciate my own husband of fifty-three years. You'd better choose your partner wisely, because you never know what's going to happen. If you're the one needing care, you'll have to count on him. If you end up caring for him, you'd better love him. I hope you have the kind of partner that I have—one who is supportive, kind, loving, smart and forever interesting."

When he was 62, Gordon realized he didn't have the partner he needed, and made the decision to leave his wife. He found it extremely hard to end a three-decade relationship, but concluded it was high time to make a change. "My unhappiness in the marriage had built up over the years, but the straw that broke the camel's back came one afternoon when my friend Ed came over. We were sitting in the garden talking, and then my wife joined us. The next day Ed telephoned me and said, 'I feel sorry for you.' You see, once my wife took a position on something, she would brook no argument. She was in possession of the absolute truth. Ed's call began a process that led me three days later to walk out of my marriage. It was the most difficult thing I ever had to do." Several years later, Gordon found a new love and the relationship lasted for fifteen years until his partner's death. Now, at 97 years of age, he looks back on this period of his life and is grateful that he gave himself a second chance. "Our years together were rich, happy and harmonious. Our love was based on mutual recognition, respect and acceptance. What she treasured most was that I made her feel she could be her best self. I know it was also true of me. She was an unimaginably powerful presence in my life and that is how I will always remember her."

Linda is 82 and has been married to the same man for more than sixty years. When she was in her fifties she came close to leaving her husband for another man and is very grateful she made the decision to stay in her marriage. "There was a man in my life who really wanted me to leave my husband for him. I didn't do it—because of my children, but also, because of my husband. We had married so young, and I didn't want to hurt him. He had been so loyal and caring, in his way. We both have very strong personalities. I appreciate his tolerance of me, and I'm tolerant of him. So my loyalty transcended the passion of this other relationship. When I started having medical problems around age 68, I knew that I had made the right decision. I've had heart surgery, colon surgery, and I was semi-paralyzed for a while—you name it, it seems I've had it. I know that my lover would not have stood by me the way my husband has. Illness changes you and it gives you much more insight and tolerance. I have been enveloped by love, and I am so grateful for the support I received from my family and my friends—and especially from my husband."

Research has found that having a stable marriage, one without serious problems, is linked to aging successfully, because it provides social, financial and emotional resources, and reduces stress.[16] But the research also shows that a bad relationship can be worse than no relationship. Certainly it can be lonely without a partner, but people in conflict-ridden marriages seem to have the highest levels of emotional loneliness.[17] And the health of your marriage seems to be intimately linked to your physical health. While a happy marriage can keep you healthy,[18] a bad marriage can make you sick, especially if you're a woman. Research found that women in strained marriages were more likely to have high blood pressure, excess belly fat, low levels of good cholesterol (HDL) and elevated blood sugar, putting them at greater risk of heart disease, stroke and diabetes. The men didn't show these same health risk factors.[19]

So, despite all the benefits that come from being in a partnership, it looks as if it's better to be alone than have the wrong partner, especially for women. And, even those who feel secure in a good relationship could find themselves single, if death or disease separates them from their partner.[20] So, since being single could be a reality sooner or later, relationships with friends and family could become even more important.

If you have found the right partner, the elders recommend taking steps now to develop and nurture the relationship by never taking it for granted, and by working on your problems. It's clear we should treat our close friendships in the same way.

Don't Take the Relationship for Granted

Jeanette knows about valuing a relationship before it's too late. "My husband's medical problems started after his retirement nearly twenty years ago, and it's been one thing after another ever since. He's had three strokes and now he has dementia and requires full-time nursing care. I'm so glad I was there for Greg when he was able to live a full life. How sad it would be if I hadn't done that. I have such wonderful memories. We didn't have much money when we were young, so we took every opportunity to entertain ourselves. Summer nights after work Greg would want to go for a swim in the river. I would call this dear woman and say, 'Would you mind watching the children for an hour or so?' And we did a lot of travelling together—in fact, every chance we could. It was good for our marriage. You should seize the opportunities when they come, so you have no regrets [later on]. The importance of having a committed relationship becomes more important the older you get."

People who have lost their spouse send us a powerful reminder to express pleasure in our partner while we still can. Trudy and her husband were 25 years old when they married. She is 86 now and recently widowed. "My husband died last year of cancer of the liver. It was really unexpected. He was dead three weeks after the diagnosis. I miss him very much; it's as though half of my being is gone. If I could be younger once more I would be ten times nicer to him than I was. This is the one regret I have in life. If you have a husband—be kind to him." Betty, who is 90 and has been a widow for decades, is always urging her friends to be kinder to their mates. "My friend complains that her husband is so lazy. I say to her, 'He's old. You know Fred has always been ambitious. If he's going back to bed it means he's worn out.' It's an awful lot more fun to live with your man than to be alone, so you should be kind to him and appreciate him."

One technique to make sure you don't take your relationship for granted is to imagine its loss. *On Grief and Grieving*, by Elisabeth Kübler-Ross and David Kessler, includes a section on regret that describes the feelings of several people who, after the death of their loved ones, grieved for lost opportunities. Alexander regretted that he didn't buy that house his wife longed for, and Josh's wife wished she hadn't kept telling him to stop singing his favourite song.

Work on the Problems

The life changes that accompany aging, including retirement, the empty nest syndrome and medical problems, can strain even the strongest relationship. The elders point out that we need to keep working hard to iron out the kinks. In this regard, Deirdre and her spouse are an inspiration. They are in their eighties and are going to counselling, as she says, "to deal with some of our issues." Several years ago Deirdre had a stroke. She says she would have been shocked when she was younger to see herself now. "Here I am, half paralyzed, and totally dependent on my husband. I thought I was going to be the type of person who was still swimming at 90. Instead, we've had to modify the house for a wheelchair, including putting in a lift up the stairs. This is something I never imagined having to do. My husband and I are companions, we are very deep friends, and I love him with all my heart. I have tried not to be such a burden on him, but we need to accept certain things about each other, and going to a therapist has helped."

There are a variety of professionals who could help you reach a deeper relationship with your partner, and a number of books that provide guided exercises. Gene Cohen, the professor of psychiatry whose work came up earlier, has written *The Creative Age: Awakening Human Potential in the Second Half of Life*, which includes a step-by-step activity plan for strengthening your relationship with your partner. Cohen suggests, for example, that you can recharge your relationship by exploring together a new activity that draws upon your complementary strengths. The approach is based on a technique called collaborative creativity, which is intended to deepen your emotional intimacy and connectedness. *Getting the Love You Want: A Guide for Couples*, by Harville Hendrix, includes a workbook and study guide. Hendrix explains that the frustrations we may have with our partner are a natural part of the differences that attracted us to them in the first place. The book includes tips about how to talk to your partner in a respectful way about the things that really matter.

Dependency on your family is not what you want, but you will need interdependency.

When I asked the elders whether they possess particular strengths that are making it easier to be old, I was thinking more of personal characteristics. While they did mention certain character traits and attitudes that are described in the next section, most of them mentioned their family as a source of strength. Their children and their children's families are a great source of caring and logistical support, and, where there are grandchildren, they are a great source of joy. The elders' experience is broadly shared. Family members form a significant part of the social network of today's seniors.[21] More than two-thirds of seniors who receive help with work around the home, running errands or emotional support, get that support from a relative.[22] The level of support strikes me as pretty intense, with about 45 percent of seniors seeing their relatives at least a few times a week.[23] But what surprises me most is the size of the family network that is supporting many seniors. Nearly a third of seniors aged 75 and older say they have six or more immediate family members (siblings, adult children or in-laws) whom they feel close to, discuss important matters with, regularly keep in touch with or rely on when they need help.[24] Since we boomers are unlikely to have these kinds of extensive family ties, all the more reason to nurture the fewer relationships we have.

Several of the elders told me they wished they had treated their family members better, and urged me to appreciate my relatives while I can. When I asked Christine, who is now 76, whether she would do anything differently if she were able to turn back the clock and be 50 years old again, her thoughts were for her mother. "I would have hugged my mother more. She was a strong woman and never complained. Our family was rarely demonstrative, but now I wish I had told her how much I admired and loved her." Deirdre finds herself dreaming about her father and the little things she wishes she had done for him. "My father loved buttermilk and I should have bought him some every time he visited. I don't know why I didn't do it. It's such a little thing and it would have given him so much pleasure. If you still have a parent, do these little things for them. Otherwise you'll dream about it later."

And when it comes to our children, Deirdre reminds us that good relations with them is in our own best interest. "Be kind to your children. They'll be choosing your nursing home." Her warning is supported by research, which found that those children who spent more time in shared activities with their mothers and fathers when they were younger provided more support to them as they aged.[25] And one of the reasons we need to be careful when choosing our parents' nursing home is that our children are watching. Research finds that they will follow this example when it comes time to determine our fate.[26] My friend Hester is sorely tempted to live this principle. Her mother lives in a large house, and Hester proposed that room be made for Hester's grandmother when she became too old for independent living. Instead, Hester's mother made arrangements for her mother to live in a shared room in a nursing home. "Fine," Hester says. "Then a shared room in a nursing home will be good enough for you someday."

Since some of us couldn't scare up enough relatives for a family picnic, let alone an elder-support network, we need to remember that people we think of as family don't need to be related to us by blood. Friends are the family that we choose for ourselves, and with changing family constellations and weakening ties, this may be the solution for some of us. Brian provides a good example. He and his wife divorced twenty-five years ago, and, although he has a close relationship with his children, they live far from his retirement home and won't be able to provide the daily help he will increasingly need. So he has created a new family for himself by bringing several young people into his life. "These were young people looking for a father. They say they met me at a time when they could have gone down a different life path. But it's a two-way street. Without these young people and their affection and caring, I could not survive. If you are not near your family, just develop your own family."

Many of the elders make a special plea for the grandparent/grandchild relationship. In previous generations, Sally's family had no connections with grandparents, and she's doing her best to change that. "If you have grandchildren you must figure out how to stay in touch. My husband never knew his grandparents. My mother's father died before she was born and I lost the last of my grandparents when I was in grade three. Our children never had grandparents. That's a terrible thing because something valuable has been left out of your life experience. We're nuts about our grandchildren. My husband never misses one of their dance competitions. It means even more to him because he never got to see his own daughter dance."

Although not a grandmother herself, Simone de Beauvoir surmised that being a grandparent was one of the great benefits of old age. "It gives them [old people] the feeling that these times in which they are living are still their times; it revives their own youth; it carries them along the infinity of the future; and it is the best defence against the gloom that threatens old age." She says the reason we are able to love our grandchildren in a "completely disinterested, wholly generous manner" is that we have neither "rights nor responsibilities."[27] These benefits flow from our relationships with young people in general, whether or not they are our flesh and blood.

Peggy Edwards and Mary Jane Sterne have written *Intentional Grandparenting: A Boomer's Guide* to help people plan ahead and take deliberate action to be the kind of grandparent they want to be. The book identifies the challenges and lays out ten child-centred principles to guide decision-making. I particularly like the advice they offer for those times when we might disagree with the parents of our grandchildren. We should hold back, listen and observe. In this way, we might just come around to their way of thinking, or at least be able to accept our differences.

Practise Forgiveness

Several of the elders urged me, while I am still able, to take the path of forgiveness in order to reconcile with family members. Susan was a war bride and she and her husband returned to England for a period of time. While there, her young daughter contracted meningitis. This was a terribly difficult period for Susan, and her brother, who lived nearby, did not support her. "I thought it was terrible that my brother didn't come to visit me when my daughter was so sick, so I ostracized him. Many years later I was going to England and I decided to visit him. I felt it was time to reconcile, and I needed to do it face to face. He was glad to see me. I now feel so much easier about him, and I'm very glad I didn't hang on to my resentment and anger."

Earlier, Deirdre talked about wishing she'd been kinder to her father, but it was her relationship with her mother that was the real stumbling block in her life. By luck, a woman several decades her senior came into Deirdre's life and helped her deal with magnanimity towards her mother. "I was about 50 years old when I met Vanessa. She became my role model and the mother I never really had. Because of her example I was able to forgive my mother. My sister still hates our mother. What point is there to that? You have to cleanse your soul of hate. We need our mothers."

Sally's father died when she was a teenager. "I was the eldest of six children and my mother was pregnant with another one. Right after Dad died, my mom's sister-in-law came to live with us to help out. That freed me, so I was able to leave home and go to college. But at the end of my second year my mother became very ill. So I had to quit and come home to take care of my brothers and sisters. There I was looking after all these children who ranged in age from a toddler to a year younger than me. So I really understand family life and the importance of forgiveness. You need to cherish your family. Give them leeway to be idiosyncratic. Don't expect them to be perfect. Don't let every little thing bother you. Just enjoy their company for who they are. Life is too short to carry grudges."

There are a number of techniques that foster forgiving and forgetting. Norah had several difficult family relationships and used a process of guided visualization[28] and meditation to work on them. Through this process she learned to be less judgmental. She told me, "I acquired an understanding that has made me less critical of myself and less critical of others. It allows me to have a good relationship with people in my emotional circle, and it makes me an easier mother." The writer Ram Dass recommends that we construct forgiveness rituals, including writing letters to those who have harmed us, or meditating upon a photograph.[29]

Keep in Touch

It was Fred's family that helped pull him through the difficult times after his wife's death. Although his sisters live on the other side of the country, he calls them weekly and is planning a visit in the summer. He says, "They're too far away for me to visit too often, but calling them once a week helps me stay in touch. When times are tough it's your family that will be there for you, so don't neglect them, no matter how far away they are." As boomers we have few excuses not to stay connected. The plethora of digital technologies, such as email, camcorders and webcams, makes it simple and affordable to maintain contact with even far-flung family members. We can share photos online and use tools such as Twitter, Facebook and websites to keep our relatives in touch with our every move.

The elders who have grandchildren emphasize that good relationships with them don't just happen, you have to work at them. Marjorie has several grandchildren, some of whom live nearby, while others reside in a distant city. She describes the efforts she makes to forge connections with them. "You need to work like mad to be very close. I phone them, visit them and invite them to visit me, and I write to the ones that are far away. When the out-of-town grandchildren come to stay we have funny, age-old traditions. For example, for special meals someone is given the task of carving the butter into a butter rose. We have been doing this in our family for four generations and it is a great honour for the little one who is given the responsibility. The girls have grown up loving our little rituals. As for the grandchildren who live nearby, I have them over to visit all the time. It is the joy of an older person's life. It keeps you young, but I warn you, carrying them around does break your back!"

Figuring out ways to stay close can be particularly important when things aren't going well for the younger ones. Lucille developed a special ritual with a teenage granddaughter who had developed some health problems and was having difficulty at school. "She came to visit with me every Friday. We had sewing projects, and while we sewed we'd have a nice time talking. She got to hear all the family stories. I felt it was a privilege to spend this time with her because I knew that, once things got better, she wouldn't need me in this way." When Betty's grandson became ill with a psychosis and was undergoing treatment, she welcomed him into her home. "He was a teenager and he wanted some space to himself. His parents knew they needed to give him some distance, but they had to keep him safe. So I said he could live with me, and I gave him a room all to himself, which is what he needed. He could come and go, and I didn't bother him, but he knew I was there, and we all knew he was safe. I'd do anything for my grandchildren."

By grieving your losses, you will suffer less from grief.

When I asked the elders about the disadvantages of growing old, they often talked about the pain of the loss of loved ones. The longer you live, the more family and friends you will lose. The elders have lost partners and spouses, some of their children and grandchildren have predeceased them, they have sat at the bedside of many dying people and they have gone to too many funerals. They worry about losing those family members and friends who remain. Elisabeth Kübler-Ross, who developed the concept of the five stages of grief—denial, anger, bargaining, depression and acceptance—emphasizes the importance of grieving in helping us to recover and live fully. She recommends that we respect the mourning process and give it the time it deserves. "Your task in your own mourning and grieving is to fully recognize your own loss, to see it as only you can."[30]

If you live a long life, there will be many times when you will need to draw on this advice. In addition to the books of Kübler-Ross, there are a number of resources available to help you come to terms with loss. *The Mourner's Dance*, by Katherine Ashenburg, explores mourning customs, both ancient and modern, which people in cultures and countries around the world have used to part with their dead. Interwoven through this fascinating book is the story of Ashenburg's daughter, who developed her own rituals when faced with the sudden death of her fiancé. Bereavement support groups can often be found by contacting your local funeral home. They may have other resources to offer, including a library of support materials. Websites such as Bereaved Families of Ontario's www.bereavedfamilies.net contain a variety of resources both online and face to face. They offer programs for different age groups, including grandparents, and provide videos that can be viewed online. The website provides links to similar agencies in other provinces and territories.

After Aunt Jean's death we held a memorial tea at the retirement home to celebrate her life and to thank the staff for their love and support. Dozens of people attended, including some family members and a friend from childhood, but the majority of the guests were members of the staff. We handed out a printed tribute that featured a photograph of Jean with her infectious grin, wearing one of her trademark hats. After people circulated and drank tea and ate cake, they took their seats in a wide semicircle several rows deep. I was hoping that people would feel comfortable telling stories about Jean and talking about their feelings for her, and I'd arranged for a handheld microphone that we could pass person to person.

Family members set the tone by telling amusing tales that had everyone laughing, and then other people felt moved to speak. There was the woman who did Jean's laundry who said, "I will never forget Jean. She told me I was beautiful." There was the receptionist who said, "Jean may have retired, but she never retired from her love of people, her love of life and her love for sharing." But the most moving tribute came from the young man who had told me earlier that Jean was his cherished friend. He told the group that Jean had been his confidante and his mentor, and her death had left a gaping hole in his life. When he spoke, his grief was so palpable that many of us were moved to tears. After the event wrapped up and people were clearing things away, the mother of the young man came over to speak with me privately. She thanked me profusely for holding the event and said, "Ever since Jean died my son has refused to speak about her. You gave him a way to share his sorrow in such a loving atmosphere and to try to come to terms with Jean's death."

Self

It may be too late to change, but now is the time to become who you are.

THE ELDERS warn me that I'll have a tough time aging well if I don't know myself, and if I can't accept myself. While this may be equally true of our younger selves, it becomes even more imperative as we get closer to the end of our life. Carl Jung writes that, once you reach a certain age, becoming self-aware is an obligation. "For a young person it is almost a sin, or at least a danger, to be too preoccupied with himself; but for the aging person it is a duty and a necessity to devote serious attention to himself."[1] Deirdre quoted the nineteenth-century French writer Stendhal on this point: *"Je vais avoir cinquante ans, il serait bien temps de me connaître."*[2]

The elders seem to feel very comfortable in their own skin. It sounds as though some of them marched to their own drummer from an early age. For others, their advancing years help to liberate them from social expectations. Gordon emphasizes that this is the single most important piece of advice he can give me. "It is difficult but essential that you do what you do for yourself, and this has nothing to do with what others expect of you." A lesson given by the early Hassidic scholar Rabbi Zusya neatly makes the point: "In the coming world God will not ask me, 'Why were you not Moses?' Instead, God will ask, 'Why were you not Zusya?'"

Bruce provides a good example of this lesson. He realized he was homosexual when he was a young man, but decided to get married regardless. "I thought I would be cured by getting married." Fifteen years later he was divorced. Looking back, he feels that his religious upbringing, with its emphasis on sin, made self-acceptance particularly difficult. But he admits that the church also gave him the lesson he needed for finding his own path. "They taught me to be guided by my conscience, and that's finally how I decided to live." For the past fifteen years, he has been in a relationship with his male partner. Bruce remembers feeling different from an early age, and this gave him lots of practice staying true to himself, while still trying to be one of the boys. "I couldn't do sports, but I could kick a ball rather superbly well. So I would sit on the sidelines reading and then do the kicking when they needed it. I needed the security of community, and in this way I was fulfilling the rules of bonding. But I didn't try to pretend to be something I wasn't." He gives this advice: "As you age, find yourself. We need to free ourselves to be ourselves; then we would hurt less. We are too attached to the public presence."

Many variables could account for the self-awareness and self-acceptance of these elders, but I found one factor very telling. Given that they came of age in an era when self-examination was not encouraged, I was struck by how many of them have made concerted efforts to explore their psychological well-being.

For Brian, therapy was the key to self-knowledge and self-acceptance. "I was born again through three years of counselling. I became aware of and accepted my abandonment as a child and wept for forty minutes. This allowed me to open up, and gave me sufficient security to go to the source of my problems. When I turned 70, I felt a great release—a joy at being freed from the needs of others. I felt liberated, and able to focus on my own needs—finally. Since this is the end run, I realize I must be able to do it my way. It's too important not to. If you want to know the key to a happy old age—avail yourself of some opportunity to get to know yourself."

Betsy first sought help from a psychologist after her husband died at a young age, leaving her with small children. "I continued to meet with my therapist for about twenty years with decreasing frequency, often around family crises related to being a single parent," she recalls. "I respected his ability to help me look at life from different perspectives. I'd call him up and say, 'I think I need a tune-up.'" For Norah it was a series of weekend workshops that gave her some valuable insights. "I became aware that one of my core beliefs was that I was responsible for all the bad things that happened in my family. When I was reading my mother's diary, I realized that she had headaches every two or three days and was in a lot of pain. I think that as a child I saw this pain on her face and internalized it as being my fault. Not until I took this workshop did I arrive at this understanding." Norah also uses a process of journaling that involves guided visualization and meditation. She credits this process with helping her to become less critical of herself and others.[3]

For Gordon, literature helped him examine his life. As you may recall, he ended his marriage at age 62. He credits one short story in particular with changing his destiny. "I had been thinking about leaving my wife," he says, "and Chekhov's 'The Lady with the Little Dog' was one of the major triggers for my decision. In the story, the hero, Gurov, comes to the following self-realization. 'Everything in which he was sincere and did not deceive himself, everything that made the kernel of his life, was hidden from other people.'[4] I felt that Chekhov was talk-

ing about me." Gordon also found support for his decision in "The Apple Tree," a short story written in 1916
by the English novelist and playwright John Galsworthy.
In this story, the protagonist looks back on his life with
regret because, in his youth, he decided to place duty
before passion. The story became an affirmation for
Gordon that he needed to change his life before it was
too late.[5]

To keep your dignity, you need to give up your pride.

Aging is a humbling experience and if we want to age
gracefully, we'll need to learn to swallow our pride. The
elders remind us that, despite our best efforts, we'll have
to face the indignities of diminished capacity, in one
form or another. As my friend who had a stroke in her
late forties reminded me, "You need to remember that
you are temporarily able-bodied."

Even Henry, who seems very healthy for 84, has his
frustrations. "Every year I make two trips with my friend,
one to ski and one to hike. Before, I used to lead the pack,
and now I'm passed by a lot of people. And, because my
friend does all the organizing, including the packing,
I've become dependent on her. I wear hearing aids, and
in the airports I can't hear the announcements. I also
have trouble on the phone, and the hearing aids don't

work at all with certain cellphones. When I was skiing, I fell and my glasses gouged my forehead, and I couldn't get through on the cellphone to get help. My friend had to make the call. It develops a dependency that I find grating."

The elders have found that a key component of self-acceptance is self-forgiveness. Betty says she has struggled with perfectionism all her life, and if she hadn't learned forgiveness she would have found aging harder. "I have had to forgive myself for no longer being able to do things a certain way," she says, "and I've learned to accept that it's not that important. Part of my problem is worrying about what others think, and I have to remember that people who are real friends won't care." Bruce advises, "If you avoid comparisons, it will help you gain self-acceptance." Richard tries to be philosophical about his diminishing prowess on the golf course: "I can't hit the ball as far as I used to, and I don't have the stamina I used to have. There is a general slowing down of your life, but it sure beats the alternative."

Reducing our worries about status and rank means that we'll be able to accept our own changed position with more equanimity. Many of the elders are excellent examples of this principle. Brian finds that his disregard for hierarchy has become a real asset now that he's older. "I treat everyone the same way," he says. "My ability to connect with people regardless of their station in life has been important my whole life. It's even more important now that I'm over 75 and really need to draw on people for help." For Henry, age is diminishing his concerns about status: "The gallows have a way of sharpening your mind. You know that you're going to cop out one of these days, so you're able to focus on the essentials. For example, I used to belong to this club, but I gave it up. There was a time when I would have thought that it looked good to be a member. Now I don't feel the same need to impress people."

The elders emphasize that getting beyond status and hierarchy will be especially important when we are considering post-retirement employment and volunteer opportunities. There's a good likelihood we may be asked to function in a capacity that doesn't have the same cachet or perks as our previous positions, and it would be a shame if we let pride limit our options. As Peter explains this situation, "I'm still working at age 75 because I like to work. In my current job there is a lack of resources and I only have the support of half an assistant. I had to learn how to use the computer at age 70. I used to have a big job, with a big title and lots of staff, and some people say this job is 'beneath me.' They make comments like, 'You've accomplished certain things, why would you do this?' But that is not the way I think. I'm an optimistic person who believes that you can improve the human situation. By doing this job, I'm making a difference and that's what keeps drawing me."

Sylvia has found that her lack of concern for status has allowed her to stay engaged in the non-profit world. She has been involved in work that supports her community her whole life and is still going strong at 84. "I do whatever needs to be done. I don't need a big office, just a corner. I don't believe in hierarchy." She says she developed her egalitarian attitude growing up in a small town. "There was no hierarchy. The managers lived right next door to the workers. We were all one community. This attitude has helped me my whole life and is even more important to me now."

As the Dalai Lama reminds us, "If you don't like what's happening in your life, change your mind." Since we can't change the fact that we are growing older, we're going to have to change our attitude about our aging self. The elders share a remarkable ability not merely to accept their situation but to embrace it. Despite the frustrations Henry experienced on his skiing trip, he is still able to celebrate his age. "I think it's fantastic to be old," he says. "The fact that you don't care if you make an ass of yourself is wonderfully liberating. It doesn't matter what people think. You need to cultivate what the French call *insouciance*."

***To retain your independence, you must learn to accept
help.***

I can see from the example set by the elders that we won't
age well unless we are willing to accept help. To retain
our independence, we'll need to let others do things for
us, and the elders seem willing to use whatever help is
required—whether household help for chores and gardening, or personal needs. They enlist the assistance of
friends, family and volunteers, and have found that there
are a variety of organizations set up to help seniors.
"There's no excuse not to get the help you need," Sally
says. "There are more and more good services out there.
Get in contact with them. Use whatever resources are
necessary."

By securing dependable help, many of the elders have
been able to continue living in their own homes. I asked
Hugh, who is 98 years old, what issues are facing him
when he looks into the future. He says that his biggest
problem is hanging on to his caregiver. If he loses her, he
will need to leave his apartment and move into a seniors'
residence or a long-term-care facility. He explains, "My
wife had Alzheimer's and we hired Sadie to work with
her. My wife died two years ago and so far I've been able
to hang on to Sadie, but she's very much in demand. I
have no relatives to help me. Hopefully I'll be able to
continue to live here with Sadie's help. That would be a

comforting thing." Betty, at 90 years of age, says that after she had a heart attack she realized that if she wanted to stay in her apartment, she'd need help. "Now I have a gal who comes two hours once a week and does a thorough cleaning. I never want to move from here if I can avoid it, so I'll try and keep getting more help as I need it." At 86, Joan and her friends rely on household help to enable them to stay in their homes. With a twinkle in her eye, she told me the following story. "The husband of a friend of mine was having an affair with the cleaning lady. When my friend found out, she had the toughest decision to make. Should she get rid of the husband or the cleaning lady? She decided to keep the husband, but, I tell you, it wasn't an easy choice."

Henry says that to prepare myself for old age, I should also identify another kind of helper—someone whose counsel I would be willing to accept. "You will need people you trust to be your personal advisers, to advise you when your behaviour is inappropriate, or simply when it makes you look older," he says. "Everyone should have a kind person who will nicely tell you what you don't want to hear. For me, it's a younger friend with whom I spend a lot of time. Many years ago I told her, 'You have to tell me when I do things that are related to aging.' As an example, sometimes I drag my left foot. My friend points out when I'm doing it, otherwise I wouldn't notice."

One of the characteristics the elders share is their willingness to use assistive devices such as canes and walkers. Pride often keeps people from using basic tools because they'd rather risk their physical well-being than appear old. The elders, in contrast, tend to put health before vanity. Doreen at 90 is not embarrassed to use a walker when she's on the street. "I use a walker because I'm not completely sure of my footing. I'm doing everything I can to minimize injury." Carol at 85 uses a cane for the same reason. "I am starting to use my cane more, such as when I go shopping. I don't want to fall and break a hip."

Gordon's attitude towards his hearing aid is a good example. I first met Gordon in a crowded concert hall at intermission when he walked over to introduce himself to me. He was wearing an oversized pair of black padded headphones that were connected to a black box that he held in front of my mouth for me to speak into. He looked like an elderly air traffic controller who had forgotten to unhook himself when he left his desk. He's 97 years old and says, "My hearing went thirty-five years ago. I have never been able to understand people who were too vain to wear hearing aids. I tried a number of different devices until I found this amplifier and it works. I'm comfortable being seen with this. Why should I care what other people think?" While he accepts his amplifier arrangement, he draws the line at a cane, which he feels doesn't fit the rest of his dapper image. However, he knew he needed to come up with a way to steady his balance, so he uses his umbrella as a cane. "I read somewhere that 27 percent of seniors die as a result of a fall. So I am exceedingly careful. I never go out without my umbrella."[6]

By learning to accept help we will increase the odds of retaining our independence. A survey done by the U.S. National Council on Disability found that 80 percent of those over 65 years of age who received assistive devices and services reported reduced dependence on others, and about 50 percent were able to avoid entering a nursing home.[7] There are a number of assistive devices on the market that could help us stay independent, and many more are in development. For failing vision, CNIB (formerly known as the Canadian National Institute for the Blind) sells talking desk clocks, wristwatches with voice capacity and jumbo-print playing cards. There is an easy-read keyboard to plug into the computer, and a voice recorder that plays back a to-do list or reminds people about important information. And for those with cognitive impairments, a number of electronic aids are being developed that could help them carry out daily activities. Tools will help them remember names, faces and appointments, find important objects such as glasses, wallets and keys, and help them remember procedural instructions, such as taking medications. The challenge that awaits us is to recognize when our limitations are chronic enough that they interfere with our health and well-being—and do something about it.[8]

But for those who are used to being very independent, relying on assistive devices or other people can be irritating. Linda, at 82, says, "I'm so dependent on my husband now. I have to hand him a jar and say, 'Would you open this, please?' When I had my stroke and I was being discharged, the nurses discussed all the instructions for my care with him, not me. He has to dole out my meds every week. It's a good lesson in humility. But it's hard to swallow. I'm a person who's always gassed up and washed my own car, and now he's doing that, plus turning it around so I don't have to back out. I have a deep sense of obligation, but it's very hard."

However, accepting help can also bring us closer to our humanity. When writer Ram Dass had a stroke, he suddenly went from being the helper to being the "helpee." He describes himself as an exceptionally self-reliant man who got his power from helping others—until he became disabled. He never fully realized just how much our culture reveres autonomy, and how humbling we consider dependency. He had to find a new way of being. "When I became dependent, I was immediately much more vulnerable," he writes. "But what I discovered was that it was my vulnerability which opened me to my humanity."[9]

To accept the indignities of aging, you need to appreciate the advantages of being old.

It turns out that there are a surprising number of benefits to growing old, aside from seniors discounts. Reduced worries are one of the big pluses. As Dan explains, "If you've managed to get this far along, you don't worry so much. You develop a certain equanimity. Even though you can't do all the things you used to be able to do, what you manage to do can be equally satisfying." Stan has found that being on the sidelines has taken the pressure off. "I'm stress free because I'm no longer in the thick of things. I'm not really competing with anyone for anything."

One of the reasons older people have fewer worries is that they have fewer responsibilities. Deirdre was a writer and appreciates the stress relief that came with retirement. "It's nice not to have to worry about deadlines anymore. As my editor once said about me, 'No matter what's going on in her life, she always meets her deadlines.' I deserve some rest now. I worked so hard. It was a tremendous pressure." As Steve explains, "There are fewer things for me to be concerned about because it's too late for me to do much in the time remaining. The worries are my children's and grandchildren's, not mine. There is a feeling of lack of responsibility."

Research confirms that the elders aren't alone in finding their lives less stressful. The majority of seniors aged 75 or over say that life is either not very stressful or not at all stressful, and a third of them say that nothing in their lives is causing them stress. If they worry about anything, it's most likely to be their health.[10]

Another advantage of old age is more control over your time. "You are mistress of your fate," Trudy says. "You do what you want, and you don't do what you don't want." One of the reasons seniors safeguard their time is that they appreciate that it's a dwindling resource. This is how Stan sees it. "Once you reach a certain age, the priorities placed on money and time reverse themselves. The money will take care of itself, but time becomes a precious commodity. Be sure you're spending your time in the way you want to spend it." Victoria agrees, "You husband your time. You want to do things, but you apply your discrimination."[11]

The acceptance of self that can come with aging often frees people from struggles to change. Georgina calls this stage *emotional independence*. "One of the benefits of old age is that you're not trying to prove yourself so much. I am what I am. I have family and friends, and other people can take me or leave me." Susan agrees, saying, "When I look in the mirror I talk to myself. I have scars and my formerly curly hair is now straight. I say to myself, 'So, you're not beautiful—you're not having to please anyone but yourself. You are what you are.'" Bruce says one reason for this acceptance is that you've run out of time. "There's no way you can reform yourself. It's over. You can stop beating yourself up." For Norah this self-acceptance has brought great happiness. "Every decade has been happier for me than the one before. You can express who you really are and let it shine out. You don't care. You can be the strangest-acting person in the world. I was singing 'Old MacDonald' in the street with a child yesterday."

The elders are too modest to say that age has given them wisdom, but they know they have acquired lots of experience, which can look like the same thing. As Marjorie says, "I have gained my authority from having lived so much. I really do know better." Georgina agrees: "You have a long memory and there is a lot of experience that informs your decisions and your outlook." As Linda puts it, "Having packed in all those experiences, it gives you, maybe not wisdom, but a little droplet of understanding and insight."

The elders remind me that, despite society's negative stereotyping of seniors, there is a certain *grey power* that comes with advancing years, and they encourage us to learn how to harness it. One of the most powerful prerogatives of age is permission to speak the truth. Simone de Beauvoir argued that this power results from society's rejection of old people: since they have been "relegated to the fringe of humanity," they no longer have to please others. "In them we see that indifference to public opinion which Aristotle called 'shamelessness' and which is the beginning of freedom," Beauvoir writes. "It means that they no longer have to practise hypocrisy."[12] Doreen agrees. "You don't hesitate to say what you think. You have more freedom of expression." Marjorie says, "I don't feel the need to spend so much time crafting what I say. I'm not as diplomatic." Sylvia adds another good reason for being honest: "At my age I have to tell the truth because my memory isn't good enough to tell a lie."

The Gray Panthers, a group founded in the United States in the seventies, promotes the role of seniors as truth-tellers. The organization was started by a group of friends to deal with the problems of retirees, grew to oppose the Vietnam War, and now has a broad social justice mandate. One of the products they sell is a button that reads "Fight Truth Decay."[13] Another organization that exemplifies the power of age is the Raging Grannies, a group of social activists, old enough to be grandmothers, who are raising awareness and political consciousness in many communities.[14] Both these groups use old age as a platform to advocate for social change—not just for seniors but for everyone, and hope to have a greater impact because of their members' advanced years. They also hope that their lined faces will elicit greater courtesy from law enforcers when they are on their protest walks or tying themselves to trees. For me they are the embodiment of the senior power described by British author Dorothy Sayers: "Time and trouble will tame an advanced young woman, but an advanced old woman is uncontrollable by any earthly force." This same description would apply to many elderly men. And you don't need to be part of a group to be an elderly activist. At 98, Hugh regularly sends his opinions to politicians. In his letters he always points out his age, and he always writes them by hand. "I like to think it has a bit of an impact. I always get answers. I find that people are polite and very helpful when they realize just how old I am."

Even on a day-to-day level, pulling the age card can elicit displays of common courtesy. When Betsy goes on the subway at rush hour she always takes her cane. "I actually do exercises every day, and I can walk quite well. But I use a cane when I'm going on the subway, especially at a busy time of day, because I think I get more respect." And Richard, at 90, appreciates that his age allows him a handicapped status for parking and gains him more consideration from fellow drivers. "I have a sticker on my car that says I'm impaired, but my only real handicap is that I move a lot slower!"

And when on public transport, many elders are happy to be recipients of the offered seat. Bill says, "The high point of being 93 is that when I'm on a crowded bus, people stand up and give me a seat." Doreen, at 90, finds that people are very courteous, especially when she looks as if she needs help. "People give me seats on the street-cars, and when I'm out on the street with my walker, people always help. I never refuse their help. They feel they've done their good deed." Henry takes any perks he can. "Someone will see my white hair and offer me a seat on the bus," he says. "They don't realize that I'm on my way to go skiing, and I'm a bit embarrassed, but I always accept. One thing you learn as you age is to trade on being older. I'm very ready to ask someone for help, and to accept help when it's offered. So I always pre-board a plane. You should exploit the opportunities."

Changing our attitude towards aging will not only lift our spirits, it may even extend our life. Researchers found that a positive attitude towards the aging process can extend your lifespan by 7.5 years.[15] Mark Twain proba-bly said it best: "Age is an issue of mind over matter. If you don't mind, it doesn't matter."

To maximize your capabilities, you should embrace your disabilities.

In coming to terms with an older self, we have a great deal to learn from the disability community and the way their members frame the issues. For starters, they see themselves as *differently abled*, rather than *disabled*. And assistive devices, such as walkers or hearing aids, are not signs of weakness or defeat: they are tools for independence.

People who have had disability thrust upon them through accident or illness can provide us with a sense of what might lie ahead, and give us some tools for accepting a changed body. Chronic knee, hip and back pain forced Val Paape to quit her profession as a yoga teacher at age 50. Her problems were the result of old sports injuries and associated surgeries. She was improving after a year of treatment when she was diagnosed with breast cancer. She explains the impact. "When my physical abilities changed, my role as a teacher changed, and I was forced to withdraw from the world of accomplishment. I no longer knew who I was. Even worse, I hated the state I was in and longed for the impossible—my past."[16] She used meditation to free herself from her self-image and to learn to love herself unconditionally. She acknowledges that the process isn't easy; however, meditation has helped her, as she wrote, to be "grounded in the process of living no matter how difficult the circumstances."[17]

Paape's removal from her profession and the accompanying loss of self will resonate with many retirees. In a recent survey, 25 percent of retirees said that their most difficult adjustment to being retired was coping with the fact that they were no longer being defined by their work.[18]

Blindsided: Lifting a Life Above Illness: A Reluctant Memoir is Richard Cohen's brutally honest account of a thirty-year battle with MS that was followed by two bouts of colon cancer. Cohen looks at the impact his illness has had on his relationship with his family, and takes some pleasure from the lesson about caring that his children have learned. He mourns the loss of his dream of being the undaunted, indestructible dad, and concludes: "The diminished man must find a way to live, though stripped of his power." It is clear from this book that Cohen has achieved his goal with grace and courage and he has much to teach us about accepting an aging body.[19]

Another resource that has helped me think differently about aging is Bonnie Sherr Klein's 2006 film, *Shameless: the Art of Disability*.[20] The film features five inspiring artists, including a stand-up comedian with severe facial disfigurement, a brilliant scholar and educator who can move only her head, and a dancer/choreographer who uses a wheelchair. You will realize when you see the film that my description, by focusing on the artists' disabilities rather than their breathtaking abilities, perverts the point. One of Klein's subversive goals in making the film was to make able-bodied people jealous of the disabled, and she comes pretty close to achieving her objective.

Klein suffered a catastrophic stroke when she was in her late forties and an award-winning filmmaker. This is her first film after her illness, nearly twenty years later. Klein's account of the journey that led her to embrace the disability community and find a home in its culture is described in her book *Slow Dance: A Story of Stroke, Love and Disability*.

You don't stop laughing when you grow old; you grow old when you stop laughing.

When I asked the elders to identify strengths that support them in their old age, they were pretty unanimous in singling out *a sense of humour*. You have to be able to see the funny side of things. As Lucille says, "I don't know how anyone gets through life without a sense of humour. You've got to be able to laugh at yourself."

Because the elders were always cracking jokes about their situation, they were great fun to be with. Here are some examples of their playful take on life.

- Bill at 93 describes his ideal tennis partner: "They have to agree to send all the balls to me, and I'm allowed to hit them back in spots where they can't be returned."
- Lucille describes life at 80: "You're on the back porch of life and one of these days you'll slip off."

- Richard at 90 says, "I take one day at a time. When I wake up in the morning, if I don't hear organ music or see flowers, I get up."
- Marie finds that it's a big problem when people discover she's 100 years old. "I know that all the time they're talking to me they are preoccupied with this one question: 'I wonder how long she'll last?'"
- I asked Malcolm, "What are the big issues facing you as you look forward to your future?" His answer: "I hope to be shot at 103 by a jealous lover." His goal? "Always leave them wanting more."
- Sylvia at 84 likes to keep the following image in mind when she thinks about old age. "I saw this sign in a grocery store. *Lost, black & white dog, left ear missing, hind leg broken, tail partly gone, answers to the name of Lucky.*"

Since we're attracted to people who make us laugh, having a sense of humour could be one insurance against loneliness. Even as our influence and connections fade with age, if we're fun to be with, it's likely that people will still want to spend time with us. Also, there is medical evidence that laughter can boost immunity, lower blood sugar levels, give our hearts a good cardiac workout, and manage pain.[21] In *Anatomy of an Illness, As Perceived by the Patient: Reflections on Healing and Regeneration*, first published in 1979, Norman Cousins describes his discovery that ten minutes of solid belly laughter, often induced by watching Marx Brothers films, would give him two hours of pain-free sleep. What made this finding so remarkable was that severe inflammation of his spine and joints had made it painful even to turn over in bed. Robert R. Provine, author of *Laughter: A Scientific Investigation*, thinks that some of the medical gains from laughter may result from being social, rather than from the act of laughing. He found that people are thirty times less likely to laugh if they are alone, so people who seem to benefit from laughter probably also have good connections with family and friends. Whether cause or effect, laughter is surely part of an enhanced quality of life.[22]

When I tell people that the elders have a sense of humour and that this seems to contribute to aging well, responses tend to be pretty fatalistic. "Well, a sense of humour is something you either have, or you don't!" I'm not so sure. I think we probably could learn to laugh more and see the funnier side of life, and there are resources out there if people want to give it a try. *The Laughter Prescription*, by Laurence J. Peter and Bill Dana, is a how-to manual designed to help develop a sense of humour, write and perform jokes, and create a lifestyle that is more playful, less serious and more humorous. The book is full of jokes and cartoons, and recommendations for other resources, including funny movies and recordings of some of the great comedians. Tips for developing a sense of humour include learning to laugh at yourself and to take yourself lightly, and the reminder that it is more important to have fun than it is to be funny. A friend of mine learned to lighten up and be less serious by taking improvisation classes.

The website for the International Society for Humor Studies, http://www.hnu.edu/ishs/, lists humour resources including books, cartoon archives and exhibits, as well as listings and links for film and TV comedies beginning from the 1920s. The organization promotes humour research through a quarterly journal and newsletter, as well as an annual conference. There are laughing groups across North America, many of them affiliated with or inspired by Madan Kataria, a former family physician in Mumbai, India, who conducted a World Laughter Tour in 1997. Kataria's practice of Laughter Yoga (more formally known as Hasya Yoga) combines laughter with yogic breathing and is based on the concept that the body gets the same physiological and psychological benefits whether the laughter is fake or real. Laughter is simulated as part of a group exercise and it turns into real and contagious laughter.[23] The principle of Laughter Yoga echoes the philosopher William James: "We don't laugh because we're happy, we're happy because we laugh."

By modifying your activities, you can stay active.

As we age, we'll probably feel like dropping activities when they become challenging. The elders urge us to resist the temptation. "Don't stop—modify" was their message. Their advice is consistent with tips for successful aging from gerontologists who recommend that we select a smaller number of responsibilities on which to concentrate our efforts. By devoting more time and practice in selected areas we can optimize performance. They call the process *selective optimization with compensation.* The accomplished pianist Arthur Rubinstein is an example of this approach. At 88 years of age he was able to maintain high-level concert performances by playing fewer pieces, practising them more often, and using variations and contrasts in speed to generate the impression of faster play.[24]

There are myriad ways in which the elders have modified their activities, rather than abandon them. Stan has curled for about ten years and now, at 80, is joining a modified curling program for people who can't bend down. "Some of my friends curl just as well with this technique. I'm not going to win any competitions, but it's a lot of fun, even though my eyes and nose run." Louise's extended family has a tradition of combining intergenerational reunions with hiking adventures. At 80, she couldn't stand the thought of not being included. "I still love to backpack, and now on these get-togethers with my children and grandchildren, they accommodate me. As long as I go at a slower pace and stop from time to time to get back my energy, I can do some of the hikes. And I don't have to do them all. I have always found the exploration of nature to be a powerful source of regeneration—and I don't want to give it up." Now that Georgina is 76 she continues to enjoy cross-country skiing, but at a slower pace. "I haven't had any broken bones, but I'm very cautious. And I find that everyone in my group is getting more cautious."

Even those who incurred injuries have worked to get back in the saddle, albeit on a slower horse. Fred switched from golfing to swimming after he developed some leg problems. He kept up his swimming once or twice a week, and now that his leg is better, he plans to get back to his golf game. Louise was a passionate skier who skied every week when she was working. "When I was in my late 70s I was on a ski trip with my buddies and I broke my hip. I had to have lots of rehab to get my ski legs back, but they're back. It was worth it!" When I met the intrepid 100-year-old Marie, she was in a retirement home recovering from two broken hips. "The doctor told me I wouldn't walk again. I said to him, 'I won't accept that.' He said, 'You wait and see.' And I told him, 'YOU wait and see.' Now I can walk with a walker. I'm an impossible patient."

Betsy doesn't like going out at night anymore and this started to interfere with her volunteer activities at her church, so she switched to daytime volunteering. Now, because she has more time in the day, she is more involved than ever. Gordon uses headphones with an amplifier as a hearing aid but the arrangement only works one on one, so in movie theatres he can't hear the audio track. His solution is to go to films with subtitles. Georgina used to love just sitting down and playing the piano whenever the mood struck her, but she doesn't feel like playing very much anymore. She realized she needed an incentive or she would end up giving up piano altogether. "Since things don't happen for me now without deadlines and discipline, I have arranged to play piano duets once a week with a teacher or a friend."

At 83 and 84 years of age respectively, Deirdre and her husband continue to travel despite the fact that Deirdre is now in a wheelchair as a result of her stroke. The airlines designate her as a carry-on passenger (which is a higher category of care than wheelchair-assist walk-on), and have accommodated them without incident. Deirdre says, "In all our travels we have never seen another carry-on. I do hate what has happened to me: not being able to walk, losing my independence. But I have tried to be indomitable. I still have the joy of reading and friends, and my love of food and clothes. My husband has not let me become a recluse. His help and the help of my children have sustained me." Gordon at 97 is still able to pursue his love of travelling by taking trips with a younger friend who acts as companion and chauffeur. He says, "I love the sightseeing and the people we meet. It's always an adventure."

At 85, Virginia says we shouldn't give up entertaining, even though we increasingly won't be able to do it the way we used to. "Keep having people into your home for drinks or even dinner. You can go out and buy everything prepared now, so there's no excuse. It's true that you can't do as much, and you'll always have something wrong with you, but the advantages are that your idiosyncrasies are overlooked. Also, if your guests are younger, they always offer to clear the table or load the dishwasher, and I always let them. My advice is—just keep going."

You will regret things you didn't do more than things you did.

About a decade ago, I heard a speech given by Edward Albee, the great American playwright, who was in his late sixties at the time. He told the audience that on his way to the event he had overheard a young woman refer to him as an "old man." This offhand comment had shaken him to the core and caused him to reflect upon his life. He concluded, "Looking back, I don't regret anything I did—just things I didn't do."

The understanding that missed opportunity leads to regret runs through the advice from the elders. Betsy's husband died at a young age and she wishes they hadn't put things off until tomorrow—because tomorrow never came. "My big life regret is that my husband and I made a dumb decision to defer enjoyment—and then he was dead. We should have pursued more opportunities for fun and friendship. That's my big advice for you. If you get a chance to do something—do it!" This is also one of Stan's regrets. "I didn't take enough risks. I regret being too timid. I was a conservative person and I always stuck to the same thing. I wish I had been bolder!"

Henry uses the following computer example to illustrate how easy it is to deny ourselves new experiences because we think we're too old. "In the office we were all using the word processing software WordStar and it was being phased out in favour of WordPerfect. They said to one of our senior secretaries, 'Why bother learning it, at your age?' I told her she was perfectly capable of learning the new software and shouldn't pass up the opportunity. She was very glad I gave her that advice; if she hadn't taken it she would have been sidelined. We should never do that to ourselves."

Research suggests that boomers are more likely to have regrets than previous generations. Life has thrown many opportunities our way. More advantages mean more paths not taken and greater chances for remorse.

Previous generations might find it easier to rationalize risks not taken or dreams not pursued because their options were more limited. Not us. So it will be particularly important for us to be self-aware when making life choices.[25] Studies find that people's top regrets centre on (in descending order) education, career, romance, parenting, the self and leisure. They surmise that these areas produce the greatest potential for regret because this is where people see the greatest prospects for change, growth and renewal.[26]

One way the elders work at minimizing regret is by actively seeking out new experiences. At 86, Joan has decided to sell her home and downsize to a condo in a part of town that's viewed by her friends as being on "the wrong side of the tracks." She chose the location because it's full of action and young people. "All my friends are moving to a staid little village that's full of people just like them—lots of walkers, canes, scooters and 'grey-hairs' lining up for all of the shops. How much fun would that be?"

For her seventy-fifth birthday, Virginia asked her husband to give her a computer. "I told him I couldn't bear having my grandchildren speaking a language I can't understand. It was such a good decision. My computer has been so important in letting me connect with everyone and keeping me up to date on everything." When he was in his eighties, Richard also decided to pick up computer skills. "I went to the library and took a few books out to figure out how it works. Now I print out my own business cards, design my Christmas cards and follow my investments. I never took a lesson."

Many of the elders hang out with young people in order to ensure they will continue to have new experiences. They join groups that have young members, take or teach courses, volunteer with youth, and spend time with young friends and family. "You won't get in a rut if you're connected to the young generation," Henry says. "I taught until I was about 80 and I was in touch with young people all the time. Eighty percent of my friends are former students, some going back to when I taught them in the sixties. It's a wonderful network of different ages. By having these young people around, I make sure I'm not generationally isolated."

Louise stays connected to youth through her grandchildren. "Over Christmas I went hiking with my granddaughter and grandson. I love to listen to their conversations and hear what is striking them as interesting. I love to see the world through their eyes. I figure I'll be able to stay forward looking if I can learn from them and benefit from their views." By staying connected to young people we'll not only ensure ourselves of new experiences, we'll also boost our morale and improve our cognitive functioning.[27]

You need to plan for the future but be prepared to seize the day.

Many of the elders didn't just drift into a successful old age, they grabbed their future in their hands. As the English novelist and playwright John Galsworthy says, "If you do not think about the future, you cannot have one."[28] The elders recommend that we envision a desired scenario, think through how to get there and then test the water before we jump in with both feet. Brian recommends planning in decades. "I've always planned ahead ten years, envisioned my ideal situation and then worked to make it happen."

This same advice came from a sample of retired people who were asked in a survey what recommendations they had for pre-retirees. They advise taking the time to envision the next phase of our lives, including our day-to-day routines, and then to make the necessary adjustments to realize our vision. In contrast, over a third of them had done no planning for retirement. A significant number of them said they were not living their retirement dreams, and they had found retirement to be very different from what they imagined.[29]

Often, when people say they have planned for their retirement, they mean they have thought about how much money they'll need, and not much beyond that. Gene Cohen found that fewer than one-tenth of his study participants, all over 60 years of age, had done any preparation for retirement beyond financial planning. He concluded that this lack of planning "undermines people's opportunities to broaden their horizons with novel recreational activities, educational enrichment, and civic engagement." Cohen emphasizes that a plan can be loose and open-ended, but it does require active exploration.[30]

Sylvia gives a very interesting example of this kind of planning. Her parents were forced to leave their homeland and start over in Canada, and she concluded from this experience that *education* and *memories* were the two things that people can't take away from you. "So one of my priorities as I get older has been to make memories," she told me. "When I was growing up we had this little cottage where we spent two months every summer, and we're doing the same thing with our children and grandchildren, and now great-grandchildren. So this is how I've been planning for my future—making memories."

Research has found that setting personal goals, coupled with a willingness to take risks, are linked to healthy aging. Simon Fraser University offered a Mental Fitness for Life program that taught seniors how to set and achieve meaningful goals, and how to take risks that would enrich their lives. Their research concluded that the workshops functioned much like a booster shot that enabled graduates to maintain mental fitness as they aged.[31]

The elders, with all their plans and projects, are terrific examples of this principle at work. Peter tells me, "Make sure you have projects—even if they're just to travel and learn." Peter is still holding down a full-time job at 75 years of age and has many volunteer commitments, so he doesn't have much time for his own projects. But they're waiting for him, if he can ever find the time. "I bought a guitar that I want to learn how to play. I've had it for two years and I haven't started learning yet, but I've got plans. Also, I want to take courses in astronomy and philosophy." At 84, Sylvia figures she has another couple of years left with the non-profit organization before she's achieved her objectives. After that, she says she would like to open a business. Gordon at 97 is busily planning for his hundredth birthday party. He has picked the venue, lined up the musicians and started inviting his guests.

But, as the Mental Fitness for Life program teaches, even as we are planning, we need to be able to seize the moment. As I thought about the elders, I realized that this principle of *carpe diem* ran through many of their lives. Although they did their planning, they were prepared to change course when opportunity presented itself. Their approach reminded me of the philosophy we adopt for whitewater canoe trips: *Over-prepare and then go with the flow.* Since a willingness to take risks is associated with healthy aging, this is probably another factor accounting for the elders' success at being old.

When I asked the elders to identify the strengths that support them in their old age, many of them emphasized this willingness to take a chance. Susan says, "I have been ready to move into new things and try new things, and this has led me into all kinds of interesting places. My life motto has been *What have I got to lose?*" She knows of what she speaks. Susan is the one who came to Canada as a war bride. After her husband retired from the military they moved several times, finally to an acreage in northern Canada. "I had never imagined as a young English girl during the war that I would live in a place like that. I loved the snow and I could see deer and moose."

Lucy relies on her motto, *It's OK, I can handle it*, to help her embrace new challenges. "People are so frightened of risk, afraid for their future security. They underestimate themselves. Take some risks. It's so important that you catch your dreams." Lucy's current life beautifully illustrates her motto: "I'm 79 years old and I have six Somali refugees living with me. This is something I never planned. Last Christmas, I received a call from someone asking me whether I could help these young men. My husband had died a few months earlier, I was living all alone, and I felt he had sent these young people to me. They were all child soldiers who had met in a refugee camp. At first I would get mad when I came home and their stuff was spread everywhere. I thought, 'I'm too old to be picking things up.' But then I'd see them all laughing together and realize that they finally have a family. They call me Mom. They are learning gradually to eat at the table with me and they even say grace once in a while."

Henry was already in his mid-fifties when he took on a new job that was particularly challenging. "It was late in my career and I was utterly happy in what I was doing, so I was reluctant to make a change. But I knew it would be good for me. As it turned out, the first two years were hell. It was really tough as I learned the ropes, but it turned out to be a fantastic opportunity. Every day I learned more and more. Although it was something I hadn't really wanted to do, it turned out to be a life-giving change." Some of the elders, like Louise, deliberately built change into their lives. "During my career I tried to change my environment every four years through being a visiting professor in various places. I wanted to be sensitized each time to what it means to be lonely, to find one's own way and to be reminded of what really counts."

Several of the elders made major personal changes later in life. At age 52, Deirdre left her husband and took out her first mortgage in her own name. "From a security point of view it was a dumb time to leave my husband, but I would do it all over again. It opened up my life to me. You must be brave." Christine fell in love with a married man when she was in her sixties. She, too, was married—to a man with a serious drinking problem. She divorced her husband to marry this new love. "Life is too short," she says. "I have never regretted it."

Gordon sums it up: "In life, opportunities present themselves and two people can see the same thing, but one will see the opportunity and the other won't. I have been able to recognize these opportunities and act on them. I regret nothing. Master your fate. It all depends on you."

Soon you won't be here, but you still need to figure out what it's all about.

While the elders told me their stories, they made continual references to the values and moral beliefs that guide and sustain them. In some cases, their belief system is expressed through organized religion; in other cases, they lead secular lives that are grounded in a sense of morality and purpose. As Peter put it, "What I do in my life is based on values, beliefs and philosophies. If you don't have these, then you get buffeted around. You must find a moral compass." Georgina agrees. "You need some form of belief system as you age. I haven't become more devoted as I age. I actually find I have more questions, rather than less. But my religion really grounds me. It's the centre of my outlook and it guides me."

Lucy's guiding philosophy is *We only become human when we reach out.* Her search for a moral and spiritual framework for her life started at a young age, and when she decided to become a nurse she selected her training hospital because of its course on ethics. Her early years of married life were full of challenges—her two sons had to have surgery and then her husband almost died—and she learned quickly to get her priorities straight. Sometimes people question her judgment, including the times she has provided a home to very troubled young people, but she has held firm in her beliefs. "An integral part of my marriage was making sure we were always welcoming people into our home and our lives. People sometimes challenge my faith, but without it, I wouldn't have a capacity for analysis. After my husband's death I found a poem he had written called 'Why Am I Here?' It's about trying to live our Christian values. You mustn't get caught in a secular world so much that you deny your own spirituality. Look inside yourself."

Many seniors share the elders' reliance on some version of spirituality. According to Statistics Canada, well over half of seniors aged 75 and over say that spiritual beliefs are very important in the way they live their lives, and about half of them attend religious services at least once a month. They say that spiritual beliefs help them to understand life's difficulties and find meaning in their lives.[32]

Only some of the elders attend religious services, but they all use some form of practice to help restore the soul, from spending time in nature, appreciating music, art or poetry, and in prayer. Some of them use techniques such as yoga, journaling, visualization and guided imagery, and working with the breath. These techniques are part of a wide range of activities that have been shown to replenish physical, emotional and spiritual energy.[33] Norah describes how she benefited from a workshop on guided visualization and meditation. "I ended up thinking a lot about my husband who was being extremely critical of me, and I had a vision of God saying to me, 'You are my beloved child in whom I'm well pleased.' It made me think that if God loves me, who am I to be judgmental? Because of the insights I gained from that one weekend I am less critical of myself and less critical of others."

Practices that focus on gratitude, such as keeping a gratitude journal and daily self-guided exercises, are another method for spiritual renewal. There are many techniques, including a daily recall of three to five things in your life for which you are grateful, itemizing the gifts you have received and the contributions you have made. A long-term research project on gratitude and thankfulness run by researchers at the universities of California and Miami is finding scientific links between gratitude practices and healthy psychological and physical well-being. One important finding is that we don't need to be "in denial" to feel thankful about our life. By practising gratitude for what we have, we should be able to stay positive and optimistic, despite being aware of the negative aspects of life.[34] This approach could become increasingly significant as we age and become sorely tempted to focus on what we've lost rather than what remains.

When we need some help feeling grateful, we can turn to a number of resources. In the book *Radical Gratitude*, Mary Jo Leddy approaches the subject as a Christian who sees gratitude as the foundation of faith in God. However, her recommendations are relevant for everyone. She says that practising gratitude "releases us from the perpetual dissatisfaction generated by the combined force of an economics of consumerism and the politics of progress."[35] She suggests we begin each day with an act of gratitude to ensure that we do not take our life for granted, end each day with trust, and fill our day with opportunities to catch our breath. In *The Gift of Thanks*, Margaret Visser argues that it is a moral flaw not to feel grateful. "Deeply felt gratefulness is a species of awe, and as such requires humility," she writes. "It implies a sense of one's own littleness before the wonders of the universe, of the earth and all of nature, of one's own life—and before the goodness of others."[36]

Several of the elders recommend books that have helped them nourish their souls. Peter suggests books by the philosopher Charles Taylor, including *A Secular Age*.

Taylor won the Templeton Prize in 2007 for his engagement in cross-cultural and cross-disciplinary questions about the role of spirituality, and he has long argued for the inclusion of spiritual dimensions in all facets of the humanities and sciences. Lucy's book choice is not surprising, given her remarkable approach to welcoming the needy into her life. She suggests Jean Vanier's book *Becoming Human.* Vanier founded L'Arche, an international organization that supports communities for the developmentally disabled. As Lucy explains, "He says we only become human when we reach out."

Another proven technique for nourishing the soul is hanging out with young people. We've already discussed the joy the elders get from their grandchildren. As it turns out, forging bonds with children is not only fun, it's good for us. A study looking at an intergenerational project involving a preschool and a retirement community found that the seniors' spirituality was enhanced by the experience; they gained a sense of relatedness to others and hope for the future.[37]

Getting old may be depressing, but that doesn't mean you should be depressed.

Although most seniors enjoy good mental health, as many as 20 percent of them suffer mild to severe depression.[38] The Canadian Network for Mood and Anxiety Treatments, www.canmat.org, has a section on the elderly that includes a simple checklist for detecting depression. Questions include the following: do you prefer to stay at home rather than going out and doing new things, have you dropped many of your activities and interests, and do you often feel helpless. After choosing the best answers to describe how you felt over the past week, your score will indicate the possibility of depression. In some cases, medical treatment may be recommended for depression. Dr. Norman Doidge explains why. "With depression, the hippocampus [the centre of emotion and the autonomic nervous system in the brain] can shrink in size and some medications can increase cell development. Without medical intervention, you're in a bad state because you can't develop new cells, and you can't learn your way out of it."[39]

Meditation is gaining acceptance as a proactive practice for good mental health, and you don't need to make a commitment to becoming a monk to get the benefits. Research has found that even limited training in mindfulness meditation can provide important cognitive tools. A 2007 study using brain scans found that people with eight weeks of meditation training were able to alter brain activity to give their overused middle brain a break. Subjects without mindfulness training continued to show brain activity in a posterior right-lateralized area, suggesting they would have difficulty removing themselves from the ongoing chatter of the busy mind, with its planning and judgments, to focus on the present.[40] Researchers feel this may explain why so many studies show mood improvement with meditation, and why, in the future, doctors may prescribe a dose of meditation rather than medicine to alleviate stress and enhance well-being.[41]

Full Catastrophe Living, by Jon Kabat-Zinn, is used as part of the program of the Stress Reduction Clinic at the University of Massachusetts Medical Center. The book is a practical guide for using mindfulness meditation to face stress, pain and illness, and provides directions on how to develop a meditation practice, including an eight-week practice schedule.

Civic Engagement

By giving to others, you will receive.

EVEN IF I didn't have an altruistic bone in my body, it looks as though I should consider volunteering, since it will likely be a path to personal success as a senior. This is one of the lessons taught by Confucius: "I sought for happiness and happiness eluded me; I turned to service and happiness found me." The elders would agree. Many of them are models of civic engagement, and the collective summary of their achievements reads like a nomination for the Order of Canada. They have contributed at the global level, including founding an international non-profit organization, and met local needs, such as reading to the very elderly. Their spheres of endeavour include working with kids at risk, bringing education to girls in remote villages in third world countries and spearheading environmental campaigns. Within the health care system their activities range from participating on boards, to setting up disease-specific organizations, to advising patients and caring for the sick. Within arts organizations, they have worked at every level, from establishing the organization itself, to board work, to being a docent. Some of them are involved with volunteer activities in their places of worship.

Malcolm sums up his philosophy: "What is most important in life are those things that you do outside of what you are required to do. Lots of people devote all their energy to work, but there's so much more. Do things that go beyond your regular job. These are the things that really mean something. These are the real dividends." This is also Sylvia's experience. "All my volunteering has helped me over the years. I'm the luckiest person in the world because everything I've done I've learned from and I get so rewarded. You give, but you also get. The importance of giving back to my community has been instilled in me since I was a child. Granny lived next door and she was always telling me how important it was to help people. My mother didn't give me advice, but I saw how she lived her life."

The payoffs that Malcolm and Sylvia talk about have been documented by research. The Harvard Study of Adult Development found that people who give of themselves for community building and guiding the next generation triple their chances that their seventies will be a time of joy rather than despair. George Vaillant calls this stage in adult development *generativity*.[1] Vaillant's findings are echoed in Gene Cohen's research, where the people who were the most satisfied with their retirement were those who had found meaningful volunteer experiences and other ways to give back.[2]

Volunteering with children seems to give seniors an extra boost. Experience Corps works in cities throughout the United States providing volunteers over the age of 55 as tutors and mentors to elementary-school children. At the same time that the program boosts student academic performance and helps schools become more successful, it also enhances the well-being of the volunteers. Seniors who volunteered with the program showed increased levels of physical, cognitive and social activity.[3]

The elders are passionate when they talk about their volunteer activities and they encourage us to select volunteer work based on what brings us joy. They point out that not all volunteer opportunities are created equal, and we need to get the right fit. Sylvia, who has been volunteering her whole life and is still going strong at 84, described how she selects her projects. "One time I was asked to head up an organization that funds a number of different programs, and I just wasn't sure it was something I wanted to do. I asked them to give me two weeks to consider. What I wanted to do was visit every one of their programs so I could see for myself. After ten days I'd visited them all and told them I'd accept the position.

I said, 'Now I can do it, because I can speak from the heart.' You need to find something you believe in and have a passion for." Sometimes the reasons that make the volunteer activity the right fit are more immediate and personal. After her son was killed in a car accident, Christine started volunteering with young men dying of HIV/AIDS. "Working with people who were losing their sons helped me heal. And doing something that mattered was really helpful. What really drives me is the knowledge that I can make a difference. We all can."

Another part of getting the right fit is finding a match with our physical capacity. At some point, failing health may give us a reason to stop volunteering, but the elders say there will probably be many things we could still do, as long as we're realistic. Despite some significant physical ailments, Norah has been able to keep up a committed level of volunteer engagement by playing to her personal strengths. "I have a type of arthritis that gets worse with both bad and good stress. Pain and fatigue really slow me down. I have one blind eye, and my sore bits jump from place to place. But there are still lots of things I can do. I like to read out loud, and I'm good at it, so I read to the elderly. Since I'm only 75, I'm a youngster to them. I used to be a teacher, so I work with a refugee family that needs help with their English. And at church I serve on the Pastoral Care Committee because they work with people with these same kind of needs."

There are a number of resources that can help us think through our options for civic engagement. The Catholic Immigration Centre has prepared a resource for potential volunteers entitled *Attention Boomers: Change the World . . . Again!: A Toolkit to Meaningful Volunteering* that can be downloaded from the website www.renaissance50plus.ca. The document has examples of ways to volunteer and techniques for finding volunteer activities. There are good tips on finding the right volunteer fit, including a list of questions that focus on the volunteer's values, areas of interest and goals. The website www.youngretired.ca provides useful information about a range of interesting volunteer opportunities, including how to apply for grants to get retirees involved with non-profit organizations.

Volunteer Canada has set up a website at volunteer50plus.ca to encourage boomers to volunteer. The site features stories exploring such issues as finding time during your workday to volunteer, fitting volunteering into a retirement lifestyle, and using volunteering to stay involved in your chosen field after retiring. Volunteer-Match, www.volunteermatch.org, matches volunteer jobs in the United States with volunteers. Even though you won't be able to use their services to find a volunteer position in Canada, you might find the website worth exploring because of its many resources to support volunteering.

By waiting until you have more time to volunteer, you may miss the boat.

If you want to find volunteer positions once you retire, you need to start practising now. You'll have to build your experience in the voluntary sector and establish a network, but acquiring the right mindset will be even more important than getting the resumé and the contacts. As Dan explains, "Being a volunteer is different from your working life because you're often doing what you do as an individual, not as a job title. You have to be prepared to do fairly simple things and to take your satisfaction from the fact that you're contributing to something bigger. You will find it hard if you wait to start volunteering until after you retire. You won't have the sense of it." William recruits volunteers for his non-profit organization, and couldn't agree more. "We have very little success with people who've never volunteered."

My friend Leslie was a senior bureaucrat who hadn't found the time to volunteer while she was working. She assumed that as soon as she retired, the non-profit sector would be hungry for her skills. But it's been a couple of years since she left work, and she still hasn't been able to make the transition. "I was used to a very demanding job and now I don't know what to do with myself. I told a couple of people I was interested in volunteering and placed a few calls. But no one called me back, so I've just let it go. I never realized that volunteering would be this hard."

I'm going to suggest that Leslie read *A People Lens: 101 Ways to Move Your Organization Forward*. The booklet was put together by Volunteer Vancouver to get organizations thinking about how they can engage the "next generation" of volunteers, and they do it by telling the stories of dozens of organizations and their volunteers. It's a terrific primer to brief Leslie on the world of volunteering, including the huge range of roles that volunteers are tackling, the variety of organizations for which they volunteer and the kind of impact the volunteers are having. After reading this, Leslie will be better able to define what she's looking for, what she has to offer and how to sell herself.[4]

Research done by the Urban Institute in the United States supports the elders' advice to start volunteering now. The study found that the vast majority of adults who volunteer while working continue to volunteer after retirement, and most who do not volunteer while working never do. However, even if you've never volunteered, the situation is not hopeless. A full quarter of U.S. retirees do start volunteering after retirement.[5]

Many of us still in the workforce feel we don't have the time to take on more responsibilities.[6] One solution would be to ask our employer to support our volunteer activity during working hours. A national survey of 990 employers found that more than a third accommodate employee volunteer activities during regular working hours. The companies believe this practice helps employee morale, and improves their public image and their relations with the surrounding community. The most common forms of employee support are adjusting work schedules, providing time off without pay and allowing access to company facilities and equipment. Companies tend to be reactive rather than proactive in offering these programs, so volunteers might need to take the initiative and approach them with the idea.[7]

The elders are proof that age is not a barrier to volunteer opportunities. Marjorie had been extremely active in a variety of non-profit organizations when she was younger and is delighted, and astonished, that her expertise is still appreciated. "My younger self would have been completely surprised to realize that, at age 77, I would still be wanted and needed on so many boards. I would have expected that I wouldn't be doing anything— that I would have completely retired." At 92, Rosemarie is still volunteering with a program that helps adults who have the speech disorder aphasia. Currently, about a third of Canadians 65 and older volunteer, and they donate the highest average annual volunteer hours of any age group.[8]

Work

To retire successfully, forget about retiring.

FOR MANY of the elders, work has been part of a successful retirement, and I suspect they would propose doing away with the concept of retirement altogether. Most of them continued in the workforce well past the traditional retirement age of 65, and they encourage us to keep working as long as we're able. As Benjamin Franklin said, "There is nothing wrong with retirement—as long as it doesn't interfere with one's work."

This is certainly Malcolm's position. "There should be no retirement except for those who are unable to work because of illness." At 84, Malcolm is still working for his employer of old—but now he's on a year-to-year contract. One of his jobs is to edit a weekly newsletter, and it's a task he loves because it keeps him in touch with his field of specialization. He warns me that if I stop working I'll age rapidly, just as the people of Shangri-La did when they left their isolated mountain paradise in *Lost Horizon*.[1] "Some of my colleagues couldn't wait to retire, but, as soon as they did, they went into decline. You must keep working and keep being productive."

Even before the recession, a growing number of Canadian seniors were postponing retirement. According to Statistics Canada, in 1997 about 17 percent of men between 65 and 69 were still working, and by 2007, that number had risen to 25 percent. In Alberta, which was experiencing an economic boom at the time of the last census, 40 percent of men aged 65 to 69 hadn't retired yet.[2] Even before the economic downturn, the boomers planned to continue this trend. When RBC surveyed employed Canadians 55 years of age and older in 2007, only four in ten planned to take full retirement, and more than a quarter wanted to retire but continue working on a contractual basis. They gave many reasons for wanting to keep working: they appreciate the income, they want something meaningful to do, they want to keep physically active, they like connecting with others, and they want to stay mentally stimulated.[3]

The elders keep working for the same reasons. You may remember Peter, who described working full-time at age 75 in a demanding job with limited resources. Here's what motivates him: "I always thought it should be the role of older people with experience to guide the next generation. I'm an optimistic person who believes that you can improve the human situation. That's what keeps drawing me." For Deirdre, work staved off old age. She was forced to retire at age 65, but negotiated teaching assignments for seven years afterwards. "I was furious to lose my job and they wouldn't be able to force me out now. I was determined to keep working and I'm so glad I pushed it. It kept my brain active and kept me in touch with young people."

At 84, William holds a senior management position and says the last thing he wants to do is retire. "The goals that people hold up for retirement are exactly the opposite of what will sustain you. '*I want to golf.*' '*I want to get at all those chores I've been postponing.*' Those things will occupy you for several weeks and then what? I believe in the value of work and what it can give you." Sylvia is the same age as William and she runs a large non-profit organization. "I was so excited when I saw they were changing the retirement age," she says. "It is really important for people my age to keep doing things. Just carry on after you reach 65—as long as you have all your marbles!"

Linda was running large non-profit organizations well into her seventies and loved the chance it gave her to stay connected with young people. "I'm 82 and when people ask me if I'm retired, I always say no. When I was well past retirement age I was asked to run an international conference. I agreed as long as I was allowed to involve students. I talked the governing body into the idea of taking wise elders and putting them on panels with the students. There were eighty countries represented. It was so exciting."

Some elders continued in full-time paid employment after age 65, others went to part-time work and some took up volunteer positions, often connected with their profession. Louise continued to work with the same employer until she was in her mid-seventies. "I loved my work and it became abundantly clear to me that I would be able to carry on as long as I continued to do my job well. It was only when the focus of my department shifted that I decided it was time to go."

After Dan retired, he was asked to take on a part-time assignment. "I asked for how long and they said four years. I said, 'That suits me fine.' Eight years later I was still there. Getting that extra eight years of work was an unexpected bonus." Henry, at 84, has been retired for a number of years, but he still has an office in his workplace. "I'm still a part of the community. I'm asked to serve on committees. I'm still involved."

Some of the elders took on new jobs when they were well past retirement age. That was when Lucille went to work for a craft store. Now, at 80 years of age, she remains close friends with the much younger woman who owned the store. "Here I was, a grandmother, and I was working full-time with these wonderful people. I had a ball. I heard once that if you're with people that are younger than you—you stay younger. The owner is like a daughter to me. The other friendships have stayed too."

Although Victoria retired when she was 62, she quickly became immersed in a volunteer program that tapped her professional expertise and focused her energies for the next three decades. "The day after I retired I woke up and I didn't know what to do with myself. I remember I walked downtown all the way from my home, a good long distance, and I don't remember walking back. I quickly got back into doing some volunteer work but realized I was going to need something more, so I enrolled in the first class of volunteers for the palliative care program at the local hospital. It became my life's work."

You need a Work Plan instead of a Retirement Plan.

None of the elders expressed regret about working too long, but some of them wished they had been able to work longer. Those who left the workforce sooner than they would have liked feel things could have turned out differently if they'd made the right moves earlier in their careers. They urge me to pay attention to the decisions I'm making now, with an eye to the future. At age 75, Betsy says, "I would like to be working now, at least part-time. I know I could be if I had developed a private practice as a social worker when I was 50, but I missed the opportunity." Betty regrets that she didn't take that refresher course that would have allowed her to work longer. "In my fifties I didn't feel I could cope with going back to school. But I should have done it. I know I could have handled it. I would have liked the work, and it would have made me very happy now to have a bigger pension."

One of the reasons boomers will need to plan ahead is that we'll have lots of competition. Many of us want to keep working, and it appears we're all angling for the same dream working conditions. We want to work Tuesday through Thursday, and mainly in the morning, from nine to noon. We want extended health care benefits, flexible work hours and a guaranteed wage. Oh, and we want 6.4 weeks of vacation a year.[4] So, if we want to command this perfect working situation, we'll need to be an attractive commodity. This probably requires some pre-planning, and we might need to pick up some additional skills.

Retire Retirement, by Tamara Erickson, includes a series of questions that can help us think through our future relationship with the world of work. *How much engagement do I want? What kind of work environment appeals to me? What level of compensation do I need? What kind of worker am I?* If we want to stay in the workforce as we age, Erickson says we'll need to develop a high degree of comfort with new technologies. We'll also need to become entrepreneurs, adept at agile experimentation, as well as negotiating and renegotiating terms of employment.

Many of us would prefer to stay with our current employer and change jobs, rather than work for another company.[5] So if we're happy where we are, we would be wise to approach our employer with a long-term strategy. There are multiple potential work arrangements, including flexible hours, job sharing, re-engagement as a consultant, or short-term assignments. It's wise to think through the full implications since they might require reworking the benefits package, or modifying equipment for an aging body.[6]

Simone de Beauvoir, writing nearly four decades ago, argues for this kind of accommodation in her book *Old Age*. She suggests that providing a worker with "spectacles" or a seat to allow him to work sitting down could mitigate some of the failings of old age.[7] As a more contemporary example, Honda Motor Co. Ltd. is testing a mechanical gadget that would ease the strain on assembly-line workers. The wearable assisted-walking device supports body weight and reduces stress on the knees so that people could get up steps and stay in a crouching position with less difficulty.[8]

It looks as though the onus will be on us to take the initiative, because few companies are taking steps to retain, attract or recruit workers over the age of 50, even though many are aware that an aging workforce is becoming a critical issue.[9] The Workplace Institute gives an annual award to the Best Employers for 50-Plus Canadians, and the 2009 award winners provide good examples for engaging senior employees. The Catholic Children's Aid Society of Toronto provides a mentorship program where former employees return as mentors to help those who are planning their own retirement. HSBC Bank Canada offers post-65 employees a pension formula enhancement; and a return-to-work policy for retirees offers contract work or regular employment, both with benefits. Seven Oaks General Hospital in Winnipeg has a project to re-engage a pool of already retired health care professionals. They also aim to keep potential retirees in the workforce through flexible retirement measures and incentives.[10]

People sometimes use retirement as a chance to start a new career. One option is what has been termed an *encore career*, a later-in-life career that combines personal meaning and social impact. In the United States, grants are being provided to colleges to create educational programs that will help boomers transition into an encore career in sectors such as health care, education and social services, which are facing a critical worker shortage. Interesting examples of encore careers are found on the website of Civic Ventures, a San Francisco–based non-profit educational think tank. A 77-year-old former independent truck driver now earns union wages in a part-time job driving people in need to appointments. A 68-year-old former executive assistant is now a part-time ombudsperson helping nursing home residents. A retired university employee now takes on temporary university-based assignments found through postings on an online resource.[11]

People who want to explore new places while checking out career options could try a short-term job adventure at www.backdoorjobs.com. Or take a holiday with Vocation Vacations, http://vocationvacations.com, and test drive a new career. The company pairs you with a mentor in your chosen field and lets you experience the job first-hand. Or consider becoming your own employer. About 60 percent of employed seniors are self-employed, and they typically retire at an older age than paid employees.[12]

Sara Davidson's book *Leap!: What Will We Do with the Rest of Our Lives?* sparked my imagination about next steps. She interviewed dozens of men and women from the boomer generation to find out how they're dealing with getting older, including the ways they are redefining their career. As she puts it, "We did not plan for this; we did not know that at fifty-five we might have thirty more years of vigorous health, lust, and a desire to contribute and create."[13] She writes that when we were younger we wanted the world to acknowledge our talents. Now, we can recognize our own talents and have

seen that the world's praise is transitory. "The imperative at this time is not to find the right job or a replacement job, but to align yourself with your purpose, with
the truth you've come to recognize about yourself."[14]

One way to discover your purpose is to think about
how you spend your free time, when you find yourself
with no external demands. Writer and mythologist Joseph
Campbell suggests looking back to our childhood as a
way of discovering our path. "What did you do as a child
that created timelessness, that made you forget time?"
he writes. "There lies the myth to live by." He suggests
we follow the advice of Carl Jung, who asked himself,
"What was the game I enjoyed when I was a child?"[15]

One person who found his purpose in a surprising
place was Michael Gates Gill, who describes the process
in *How Starbucks Saved My Life: A Son of Privilege Learns
to Live Like Everyone Else*. Gill has found happiness and
fulfillment working at Starbucks after being pushed out
of the advertising industry. His story is a perfect example of finding the job that fits the truth you've come to
recognize about yourself. Gill says the job saved him:
"Saved me from my pursuit of empty symbols, but also
my anxiety about a fear-filled superficial life that hadn't
been, in the end, helpful or even enjoyable for me."[16]

Home

To keep a home, consider leaving your house.

L ISTENING to the elders, I can see that one of the toughest decisions I'll be facing is where to make my home. They warn me that my decisions must be timely; otherwise, I could reach a point where I no longer have the capacity to choose for myself, and others will make decisions for me. What motivates the elders to stay in control of their fate is a desire to maintain their independence for as long as possible, and a wish not to be a burden on others.

One of the most compelling teachings from the elders is the lesson to simplify our living arrangements. Most of the elders have downsized, and none of them regret that decision. One of the big benefits of reducing your living space at the right time is that it increases your odds of being able to live in a space of your choosing. Linda and her husband downsized from a three-level to a one-level home. They were both 80 years old when they made the move, but they had been planning it for years. The reduced demands of the simpler house have meant that Linda has been able to continue to live in her own home, despite her physical limitations. She admits, "I suppose this is just a stopgap, but I'll just try and keep getting more help so that I can stay here. I can't imagine leaving here. I can't even go there in my mind. I just love my independence."

Several of the elders were motivated to downsize from the family home after the experience they had with their own aging parents. Five or six years ago when Dan was in his late seventies, he and his wife sold their home of twenty-five years and moved into an apartment. "My wife was pushing me to do it. We had to look after her parents as they aged, and it was hard because they lived in another city. Then her dad died and we had to close down their house and move her mom to a home near us. We're not going to inflict that on our kids. As you get older you need to move into a place that runs itself. We don't want our children to be looking after us."

Sylvia's decision to sell their home was also motivated by wanting to ease the burden on her children. "We downsized ten years ago when I was 74 because we didn't want to leave the house full of stuff as a legacy for our children. We cleared out a great big house and moved into a condo and it was a great relief to have it done."

Norah remembers how painful it was to clean out her mother's house after she died. "I was all alone with no one to help me, and I had a very difficult time. I gave things to forty-three individuals and institutions, including museums and archives. It took me months and months."

Other people downsized because of illness. This was Betty's story. "Twelve years ago at age 78, I had a cardiac arrest. They kept me in intensive care for a week. After I got out of the hospital I went back home and I cut the lawns that summer and did the garden. I knew it was too much. When November came, I decided it was time to sell and move on. I moved into a three-bedroom apartment that wasn't far from where I lived, so I wasn't leaving my friends. I told myself that I was very lucky to be moving anyplace. By adopting that attitude I helped myself immeasurably."

For some, their move was particularly well timed. Four years ago, when Jeanette was 78, she and her husband gave up their home and moved into a one-level condo. This proved a godsend since Jeanette's husband developed serious medical problems after he retired. "He's had three strokes and is now in a lodge only ten minutes away. He's very comfortable and I can visit him daily, but now I'm living by myself. I'm so glad we moved when we did."

Based on the elders' stories, it seems that if we haven't downsized by the time we're 80, it's probably only illness or the death of our spouse that will force a change. When Trudy was 84, she and her husband left their home of fifty years and moved into a retirement residence. "Up until then, we'd been able to manage in our home. We had medical problems, but we coped by hiring a house-keeper and making some modifications to the house, including adding an elevator. But then I dislocated my hip for the fifth time. The housekeeper didn't work nights, so in order to go into the hospital for surgery I needed to find someone to take care of my husband. I knew he wasn't safe on his feet and I was very afraid of him being alone and falling. So we moved together into a retire-ment home. I thought it would be temporary and we would be able to move back home after I recovered from my surgery. But there were complications, and I was in the hospital for three months. After that, I could see that I wouldn't be able to take care of my husband, so we decided to sell the house. The housekeeper worked with me to pack up the whole place. I sat and directed her because I couldn't move."

Richard was 90 when his wife died. He saw no point in living alone in their home, so he sold the house and bought a small condo. "We'd lived in that house for fifty-three years, but once my wife was gone, it wasn't hard to leave. Because I had a handyman and a gardener and a cleaner, I didn't do much around the house anymore anyway. This coming winter, if my daughter invites me,

I'll go to Florida for five to six weeks. This place has no worries—all I have to do is lock the door and leave."

Deirdre and her husband are in their mid-eighties and have steadfastly resisted their family's efforts to help them move to an apartment. They are committed to doing whatever it takes to stay put. Since Deirdre had her stroke, this has meant hiring help and installing a lift on the stairs so she can go up and down to their bedroom on the second floor. Deirdre knows that living on one floor would certainly make their life easier, but she can't bear the thought of giving up her home. "To me home is somewhere I'm embraced and feel safe—something that will always be there."

Although several of the elders relocated to another city after retirement to be closer to family, or to get away from the snow, most of the elders stayed in the same city. However, we retiring boomers seem to be considering a broader range of choices for retirement living than previous generations—just because we can. A 2008 RBC poll of Canadian boomers found that about 40 percent would like to retire somewhere other than their current community. The most popular places fell into the following four categories: nature communities with outdoor activities, places with many social activities, healthy-living communities and environmentally responsible communities. While the survey results asked respondents to pick their favourite option, I, for one, would like all of the above. More than three-quarters of the boomers said they were not attracted to seniors-only communities.[1]

Where you live will determine whether you can live well.

The elders have very definite ideas about where we should be living if we want to age successfully. One thing they emphasize is a place with lots of stimulation. At 86, Joan is the one who bought a condo that, according to her friends, is "on the wrong side of the tracks." Her new condo is in a lively development with lots of young people, families with small children and a nearby farmer's market. "I went for this area because it makes me feel years younger, unlike that dull part of town where my friends live that I call 'blue-rinse village.'" Betty, aged 90, lives in the "heart of the action" on the main street of her city, in a prime shopping and entertainment district. "I broke my wrist and my pelvis, and when I was in the hospital I said to my friend, 'If I live through this, I'm going to move downtown.' I kept my word and signed the apartment lease in the hospital. I moved in here three weeks later to the day. I love living here. It's so much fun. There's always something going on and it makes me feel so alive. I hope I never have to leave." Gordon, at 97, loves his perch in a downtown hotel where he's lived for decades. "Living downtown is so much better than living anywhere else. And living in a hotel is the very best thing because I feel part of ongoing life and it's never boring. And it's easy to walk when you live downtown. I walk three miles a day."

When Brian decided to build the retirement home of his dreams, he made the mistake of selecting an isolated location. "I wasn't thinking enough about stimulation when I built my first retirement home, I was thinking about the spectacular view. Everything was fine until the building was completed. Then, I no longer had a project and I started to wonder how I was going to keep my brain alive. I hadn't realized that the splendid isolation would come at a cost. The lack of intellectual stimulation left me with a feeling of emptiness. I knew I needed the social engagement and realized I had to move." Now he has crafted a highly satisfying retirement life surrounded by friends, including a group that meets regularly called the "Golden Oldies." He sums up what he learned. "After you reach age 75, you need to be living where you have easy access to a hospital, an airport and a social community. You need to be thinking about this when you're in your fifties, and still have the physical well-being to make it happen."

According to Lucy, the presence of children should be a prime criterion for choosing our location, so this rules out retirement homes for her. "When Nelson Mandela was asked what he missed most about being in prison, he said, 'Being with children.' This is what worries me about retirement homes and communities. The boomers don't have time to spend with the seniors, and there are no children anywhere. So there is no contact with the younger generations."

Lively locations also mean access to medical help. At 84, Henry still uses his country home from time to time, but has rented an apartment in the heart of the city. "I am using my city home more and more. I subscribe to a Lifeline medical service in the country that will alert my neighbours if I am ill. But I am two miles from the nearest neighbours, so at some point I will need to give up country living."

Another reminder from the elders is that we're going to limit our independence if we choose to live in a place where we need to depend on a car. We'll also find it harder to get exercise. What we should be looking for is a location where we can get around by walking, biking and using public transit. Although many of the elders are still driving, when they selected new living spaces, they looked for access to public transit and pedestrian-friendly environments. Betsy has just purchased a condo near a bus stop. "I may want to give up my driver's licence at some point, so public transit is very important." Judy decided to sell her car when she moved to a new city to be closer to her family. "I picked a conveniently located apartment building and learned to ride the bus. I made the choice to get rid of the car because if I didn't, I knew

I'd never walk. This way I also got to know the city. It's a lot easier to do that on foot."

I asked my friend the rural doctor what he thought about this advice from the elders. Their recommendations seem to rule out a future of rocking on the front porch of that beautiful country home, or sipping cocktails at sunset on the dock of that winterized but remote cottage. Patrick is the kind of old-fashioned doctor who makes house calls to the scattered farm homes in his district, and many of them house elderly patients. He has lived in the country for his entire career and loves the way of life, but he says the countryside is no place for the elderly. "I've seen way too many frail people who could be doing so much better with more support and stimulation. Yes, there are the exceptions, but most of them shouldn't be so isolated. And I worry about what will happen when I retire. Will the next doctor make house calls?" In preparation for their own retirement, Patrick and his wife have bought a condo in the heart of a nearby city.

There are a number of useful resources to help you think about where you're going to age. Richard Florida's book, *Who's Your City*, has a section devoted to the location needs and priorities of empty nesters and retirees. He argues that choosing where we want to live is probably the most important decision we can make in determining our happiness.[2] To help identify the best place to live, Florida has developed a series of variables to consider, organized in five broad categories: opportunity, basic services, leadership, values and aesthetics. There are also a variety of online tools to help think through location options.[3]

Another resource is *Retire in Style*, by Warren Bland, a geography professor at California State University. Bland has compiled a Top 60 list of best places to retire in North America, with several Canadian cities making the top ten. Bland rates the cities on the following twelve criteria that retirees should consider when making their decision: landscape, climate, quality of life, cost of living, transportation, retail services, health care, community services, cultural and educational activities, recreational activities, work/volunteer activities, and crime rates and public safety.

Once people identify a city that interests them, Richard Florida's "place finder" (whosyourcity.com) helps them compare where they currently live with the relocation option. Florida adds some more intangible but equally important criteria to those identified by Bland, including connectedness, political leadership, business values, diversity, access and engagement, tolerance, trust, self-expression, people climate, beauty, unique character, lifestyle and buzz (energy level). He suggests you pose questions such as: "Do people generally trust one another?" and "Can you be yourself wherever you are?"

If you decide to strike out for a new location later in life, these questions are extremely important in determining whether you will truly feel at home. You will have to create a strong emotional circle to support your elder years, and will need enough time and energy to put the foundation in place before you need to draw on it. It's not unusual for people to form new circles of support after retirement. In *Twelve Weeks in Spring*, June Callwood describes the way sixty people formed a care team to allow Margaret Frazer to die with dignity at home. Margaret was 68 when she was diagnosed with terminal cancer. Because she was single and her family lived far away, she would have died in hospital if not for her emotional circle. Margaret had retired from teaching when she was in her fifties and only then became active in church and volunteer activities. The people who comprised her care team were all people she had met post-retirement through these organizations, and many were simply acquaintances, rather than intimate friends.

Aunt Jean is another person who created a late-life community. During the three years she spent in her retirement home, the wall next to her easy chair became an ever-expanding mosaic of photos of her new friends—the caregivers and staff. Over the years I was bemused to watch the photos of her family gradually being relegated to the background, while the snapshots of "Jean with Juanita" and "Jean with Maria" took centre stage.

This was Jean's immediate community of caring, and by acknowledging her new family in this way she was expressing her love and gratitude, and cementing their affection for her.

One approach to finding a late-life community is to rediscover your roots. Gerald Hodge's book, *The Geography of Aging*, tells the story of Mohammad Qadeer who decided in his senior years to turn to his ethnic identity for social sustenance. Qadeer's previous community had been primarily made up of people with whom he shared professional and political interests, but he decided that retirement was the time to make a new start in a new place. He and his wife left the small town where they had raised their family, moved to Toronto and developed a social network largely comprising "co-ethnics." "With more of my life spent in Canada than in my home country of Pakistan, I do not regard myself defined by my birthplace. But I now meet my current needs for companionship primarily through my ethnic network."[4] If you don't have any strong religious, cultural or ethnic roots, you might want to develop some, particularly if you decide to enter a retirement home. Some homes are organized around a particular cultural community, and provide staff who speak the language, include ethnic foods on the menu and encourage cultural activities and the observance of religious practices. Because of the resources, financial and otherwise, that these specialized residences are able to attract, the services and facilities they provide can be of superior quality.

Designing for the future could ensure you'll have one.

Our choice of living space will determine how long we'll be able to stay in our home, and the elders encourage us to make the design choices now that will work for the long term. They pretty much speak with one voice about the need to keep it simple, with smaller-sized living spaces requiring minimal maintenance. As Joan puts it, "Don't get involved in over-gardening or having a house that's too big." Also, light will become increasingly important as we age, and if the elders have a design concept it is *sunny and airy*. As Betty says, "My apartment gets lots of light and I didn't want to lose any of it, so I didn't put up any window coverings. Dark places are more and more depressing the older you get. It's very important to understand the impact of your surroundings on how you feel."

When Brian had to relocate and build another retirement home, he figured he'd learned his lesson, so he thought long and hard about all the practical requirements of old age. "The entire house is completely accessible. I've designed it so that even if I were to be in a wheelchair I could get in and out of the house, and into and out of the car—all by myself. I could still sit on the balcony and look out onto the garden. The lower level is completely self-contained so I rent it out now for extra income, but it would make a good space for a caregiver, if the time comes."

When Judy reached her eighties she realized that her walking was deteriorating, and she was going to need an increasing amount of personal care. She hated to give up her independence, but knew she wouldn't be able to stay alone in her apartment for much longer. Her daughter came to the rescue by adding an extension to her house for her mother's use. Judy's large room functions as a bedroom/sitting room, complete with adjoining washroom, and a small kitchen bar with a microwave and bar-sized fridge. The unit was designed to be completely wheelchair accessible, right down to the garden beds that were raised to chair level. Judy is now 95 and has been living in her apartment for over a decade. "This set-up works perfectly because it gives both me and my daughter's family lots of personal space. I have a helper who comes every morning except Sunday. She gives me my bath, and she dusts and looks after the apartment. My daughter does my shopping and the meals. The apartment design works in every respect except for the kitchen tile, which is so strong that glass shatters when it falls.

This is very dangerous. I love the garden and the sound of the pools. The only thing I miss from my old life is bridge. I can't get a foursome here."

People in the process of building or renovating their home should build in "Senior-Smart" features. By keeping the windows low, they'll be able to see over the windowsill if they're in a wheelchair. By strengthening the surrounds around the bathtub, they'll be able to install grab bars, if required. By widening the doorways, they'll be able to navigate a motorized scooter through the house. I was impressed by a home I toured in Victoria, British Columbia, that was being built for a couple in their mid-eighties. At the moment they are both very fit, but they designed the house with an eye to their long-term residency. All doorways are wide enough to accommodate wheelchairs, and the doors are pocket, rather than swing closing, for greater mobility. Steel supports surround the bathtub and shower so that grab rails can be easily added, but only when they need them. The couple told the builder they don't want the handrails installed right away. They don't want the place to look like a seniors' home—at least, not yet. They have included a separate living space that could be used for live-in help. Being able to offer accommodation might increase the odds of attracting employees in an increasingly competitive marketplace, and could make the help more affordable. For now, the room with ensuite bathroom serves as a guest suite.

The Safe Living Guide: A guide to home safety for seniors, available from the Public Health Agency of Canada, is a helpful resource for thinking about senior design features.[5] CMHC (Canada Mortgage and Housing Corporation) offers the Residential Rehabilitation Assistance Program and the Home Adaptations for Seniors' Independence Program that provide financial assistance for home adaptations that will help low-income seniors perform daily activities in their home.

To think long term, we need to follow the research on intelligent homes coming out of places like iDAPT, the Toronto Rehabilitation Institute's facilities for Intelligent Design for Adaptation, Participation and Technology, www.torontorehab. com/research/idapt.htm. The goal of the lab is to design artificial intelligence systems for our homes that would recognize when we need help and prompt us with instructions. We could be reminded to take our keys with us when we go out the front door, or to turn off the stove before we leave the house. The system could recognize signs of trouble, such as when we've fallen, and place a call for assistance. Motion-activated lighting could provide lit pathways to the bathroom at night, and motion-activated faucets would assist arthritic hands. If we become hard of hearing, oversized speakerphones could help us communicate with people at the door or on the phone. By incorporating some of these features in our living space, we should be able to extend the period that we are self-reliant.

In addition to modifying our own private living space, there are many other housing options for boomers to consider as we age. For example, some of my friends talk about getting together to form a co-operative living space where like-minded people could share accommodation. Another approach is offered by Abbeyfield Houses Society of Canada, www.abbeyfield.ca, a not-for-profit organization that offers rental accommodation in homes that are supported by a professional house manager, and provide home-cooked meals and 24-hour emergency services. Their goal is to offer a warm, family-style house with a balance between privacy and companionship, security and independence. Alternative Living for the Aged, www.alternativeliving.org, operates exclusively in Los Angeles, but they provide an interesting model. The non-profit agency provides affordable housing for low-income older people as alternatives to living alone or institutionalization. They also encourage seniors to share housing by offering a free housemate-matching program that uses counselling and personality profiling to pair you, not just with other seniors, but also with mid-age and younger people.

If you don't control your things, your things will control you.

While the elders' ideas about simplifying our living space make great sense, many people have too much stuff to put the idea into practice. This is probably the biggest reason people don't want to downsize—they can't face dealing with all their possessions. "I have so many friends who say they can't move now—it's too late," Dan says. "They have accumulated so much stuff, and they don't know what to do with it." However, this same concern was a motivating force for many of the elders. They decided to downsize, or at least de-clutter, because of the burden their accumulation could place on others. As Steve says, "We've been in this house for thirty years and we're getting rid of stuff. We're thinking of the people who, otherwise, might have to clean it up."

The elders have used a variety of techniques to pare down, including hiring professional de-clutterers. They have donated papers, books and historically significant items to archives and museums, and in one case transferred deed of their home to an educational institution. Georgina has found the process liberating. "Now that I've cleared so much stuff out, I see things differently, and I don't want clutter everywhere." The elders' example has inspired me to tackle my own de-cluttering. I've started donating things to people or organizations that could put them to good use, and I'm calling it "The Creative Give-away Program." So far I've given away several pieces of art, some jewelry and a specialized book collection. The process I've set up is half the fun. To identify the appropriate recipient, I establish my criteria, and then canvass the landscape to see who qualifies. For example, I wanted to donate my Northern and Inuit collection of some seventy books to an organization where the books would see a high level of use by Inuit researchers. By contacting a number of experts I received several recommendations, and I selected an educational institution that is putting my books to much better use than I was.

Like the elders, I feel guilty that if I don't clean up my own mess, I'll be placing an enormous burden on others. Also, I can see from my give-away program that family or friends are unlikely to donate my things as effectively as I can. They may not understand the value of some of my possessions, nor have the professional contacts to advise them. But one of my biggest motivators for starting to divest now came from an unlikely source. Two years ago I saw a large colour photo in the newspaper of a man with a stricken face standing in front of his deceased father's collection of miniature liquor bottles. There were eight thousand of them. The son had been left to dispose of the collection, which had turned out to be an onerous task, and one he resented. "He [Dad] should have taken care of it when he was alive," the son said. But the most memorable part of the story was the son's insight into the problem: "One thing I've learned is that whatever you think you have of value, it's garbage to the next person."[6]

Another reason for giving things away sooner rather than later is to take pleasure in the gifting. Norah spent months clearing out her parents' home, and now she is worrying about what to do with her own possessions. "As far as I'm concerned, my sister-in-law made a big mistake when she decided to sell her entire collection of 140 paintings. First she should have seen if anyone in the family wanted them. That's what I'm going to do. I'm going to give my things away now, and just keep a photograph for myself to remember them. Take my china, for example. I find entertaining harder and harder, so how many beautiful plates can I use? Next Christmas I'm going to give the twenty people in my immediate family the chance to select their own present from among my things."

Another reason for starting soon, as Norah realized, is that you need to have your wits about you to be able to handle the de-cluttering effectively. "Mentally and physically, it's an arduous task to deal with all these things. I now give books away right after I've read them. That's easy to do. But it takes brains to sort through the years of accumulated things."

There are a number of resources to help us get rid of clutter, including companies that make a business out of helping us store, winnow down or organize our things. But to get at the roots of our desire to accumulate, we should spend some time with Duane Elgin's book *Voluntary Simplicity*. Elgin's goal is to help us develop a life that is outwardly simple and inwardly rich, and he explores a philosophy of simplicity that includes appreciating life and living more voluntarily (i.e., acting in a self-determining manner). He says that living a life of conscious simplicity will result in more balanced consumption, and he includes some consumption criteria to help us get at the root of why we buy what we do. As examples: "Are my consumption patterns basically satisfying, or do I buy much that serves no real need?" and "How tied are my present job and lifestyle to installment payments, maintenance and repair costs, and the expectations of others?"[7]

For many of us, the biggest struggles are around getting rid of things that connect us to family history or remind us of deceased loved ones. Here is where Beth Powning's novel, *The Hatbox Letters*, can be a real comfort. Powning's book is a meditation on memory, mourning and loss, and beautifully illustrates the complexities that underlie our attachment to things. Kate, the 53-year-old widow who is the story's narrator, describes her memories of a time she was 18 years old. At one stage in her story, both her adoring and adored grandparents have died and the family is selling their home and emptying its contents. Kate had made a collection of her grandmother's things, including her rolling pin, her potato masher and her little paring knife. "But when she'd looked into the box, she'd realized that Granny was not there. It was just a collection of things. . . . A collection of things that once disarranged loses its magic."[8] By working through all the layers and interweavings of longing, regret and love, Kate comes to understand that loved ones cannot be found in things. This book makes it a bit easier to get rid of our stuff by helping us understand why it's so hard to do.

Body

If you're lucky enough to live a long life, you won't be healthy.

WHEN I BEGAN the process of interviewing the forty people who had been recommended to me as role models, I assumed they would all be in good health. I thought that a vibrant old age would be free of health problems and medical challenges. Turns out that I was laughably wrong, as the medical histories of the elders showed. Now, my more realistic understanding of our medical future runs like this: *If you're lucky enough to live past age 75, you're going to have health problems.* What the elders share is not perfect health, it's a determination to live life fully, despite a failing body. As many of them put it, "Being my age means I have to deal with health problems—but it sure beats the alternative."

According to statistics, by age 65 one in three of us will have a disability, and by age 75 that number will increase to half. These disabilities will likely be mobility and agility limitations, often accompanied by pain. Many of us will have difficulty with our hearing, some form of visual impairment and memory loss.[1] And once we're over 75, nearly a quarter of us will need home health services to help us with the activities of daily living.[2] Even if we're able to stay high functioning to the end, we'll still feel the daily irritations of reduced ability.

The upside to this downside is that seniors seem to accept their diminishing health status with equanimity. In a 2003 Statistics Canada survey, 63 percent of those aged 85 and older reported that they were in good to excellent health. At the same time, two-thirds of all the seniors in the study who were over 65 reported at least one chronic condition, including arthritis and rheumatism, high blood pressure, back problems, heart disease, and vision and hearing problems. And the older the senior, the greater the prevalence of these problems. The women had more chronic conditions than the men of the same age.[3]

Let's take Betty as an example. She's the 90-year-old dynamo who lives by herself in an apartment in the heart of the entertainment district. Her social schedule is so busy it was a challenge for her to squeeze in our interview. Here is how she describes her medical history. "I had a heart attack when I was 78. A few years ago I broke my wrist and my pelvis, and I was supposed to have a walker, but I never used it. I've broken my hip. I have pins in my wrist because I've broken them both twice, and I've had a rib out on each side. I've had the odd fall where I've fallen backwards. I've crushed some vertebrae and had a big growth removed. I had a partial replacement to extend the life of my hip. I've had bowel surgery. I have osteoporosis and high blood pressure." And then there's Richard. He's the energetic 90-year-old who plays golf fanatically, travels to Florida in the winter and moved into an apartment last year after his wife died. Here's his medical story. "I had a stroke when I was 67. I lost the use of my right arm and I had to relearn how to write and spell. The doctor reamed out the artery to my brain. He told me it was a risky procedure, but it was successful. It happened in February and I was back playing golf in May. Then, when I was 74, I had an aneurysm of the aorta. I survived that and I still have the plastic pipes installed."

While many of the elders have survived these kinds of major medical crises, most of the physical problems they face are not life-threatening—just irritating, frustrating, painful or all of the above. As Brian put it, "The problem of old age is the physical running down of the plant." Peter gives some examples. "My strength and my speed are diminishing, and some of my bodily functions don't work as well as they used to. I have to take medication for my prostate, and I urinate more frequently." This is

Henry's problem too. "I have to pee more often. Every time I see a toilet, I use it." Victoria lost her sense of taste and smell when she was in her early eighties. "Evidently these parts just wear out. One day you wake up and your system has decided that you're not going to taste or smell. It has really spoiled my interest in eating!"

Diminishing energy levels are a common complaint. As Malcolm says, "Getting old is about getting tired. My stamina isn't what it used to be. I'd like to be able to do more and stay awake a little longer." Marjorie agrees. "I am slowing down. I'm so affected by weather now. I get tired. I don't sleep all that well. My back is not that great and my left leg is not what it should be."

The tough part is that you can't boss your body around the way you used to when you were younger. Trudy says, "You never know how you'll wake up. You may be on top of the world and capable of doing whatever. Or you may feel like crawling back into bed. Certain organs have a mind and a will of their own." Susan finds this too. As you may remember, she is a quilter. "I love to sew," she says, "and sometimes I feel frustrated at my lack of energy. I'm working away on my quilt, and then one hour later I wake up. I've just nodded off, despite my best efforts. I get mad at myself."

Many of the elders suffer from the aches and pains of arthritis. Linda describes these frustrations. "I have painful arthritis in my hands and can't open jars any-more. So I ask myself, 'Why am I alive?' I guess I'll just carry on and keep doing what I'm doing. You do expect as you become older that you'll become ill, but I didn't expect this pain in my hands."

A shared frustration is not being able to anticipate how you're going to feel from day to day. Betsy explains that you can't count on an aging body: "Your body lets you down and you never know when it's going to happen."

If you give up on your body, it will give up on you.

The elders urge me to work at maintaining my physical fitness through sports and exercise and they warn that if we give up on our body, it will give up on us. Peter offers this cautionary tale: "I had a friend who was a futures trader and when he turned 40 he started referring to him-self as 'Old Harry.' He became overweight, and smoked and drank too much. He died when he was 45." Dan has seen similar problems. "Some of my son's friends who are in their fifties are not in as good shape as me, and I'm 83. That's awful. Is it too much TV, or being totally obsessed with work? This is very wrong. People who don't work at staying in shape are in for trouble. What continues to pay off for me are my exercise and my sports. I'm not a sporting person, but I do enjoy downhill and cross-country skiing, canoeing and tennis. I've been doing them all my life, and I've just kept doing them. My wife is arthritic, but she's going to keep going to her exercise class if it kills her."

Like Dan, most of the elders led active lives when they were younger, and they continue to do so, even though it doesn't come as easily. As Susan says, "Now that I'm getting older, I have to force myself to keep going out. I find it tough, especially with my osteoporosis. I could lie on the couch and the pain would go away, but I push myself to go out and walk." Louise was a passionate skier and at 80 continues to push herself to stay active. "My hip and knees hurt when the weather's bad, but I'm determined to stay mobile. I do exercises daily, and I walk every day for half an hour at least. I never take the elevator to reach my apartment, I always take the stairs." Research shows that the elders are right to keep making the effort. A Swiss study that looked at young-olds (aged 64–74) confirmed the link between well-being and participation in sports and physical exercise. The results determined that exercisers feel better, and that quitters, those who used to exercise when they were younger and gave up, show a much lower level of well-being.[4]

Listening to the elders, I got the impression that if you hadn't been physically active in your youth, it was now too late. But it turns out we'll need to come up with a better excuse, as research shows that it's never too late to gain benefits from exercising. As soon as you start moving, you'll become healthier and you'll feel better. And to take it one step further, we may be able to reverse the aging process. Research supported by the U.S. National Institutes of Health (NIH) found that resistance exercise, such as working out with weights, actually reverses muscle aging at the genetic level. After six months of resistance training, older adults were able to improve their capacity to lift weights, and the improvement extended right down to the muscle-building blocks. It seems that weightlifting might reactivate genes that protect muscle cells from damage, and improve cell functioning.[5]

To maintain what health you have, you need to admit when it's failing.

The elders urge us to be proactive about health in ways that go beyond exercise. This means eating properly, having regular checkups and taking all the recommended tests. As Peter says, "Looking into the future, lots of things are out of your control, but one thing you *can* do is take care of yourself physically." Older people need to get really good at listening to their bodies and paying attention to things that need fixing. After Stan broke his foot, he was in constant pain for months and he refused to accept his doctor's diagnosis that this was going to be a lifelong condition. "I kept searching for second opinions. Finally I found a physiotherapist who figured out how to support my broken foot with proper orthotics, and he straightened my back. Now there's no more pain." As mentioned earlier, the writer Ram Dass had a stroke at 65. He feels that one reason for the stroke was that he had been ignoring his body. He kept forgetting to take his blood pressure medication. Then, when he was diving in the Caribbean, he got some clear signs that something was wrong, but he refused to listen. "By overcommitting myself, never saying no no matter what my body was telling me, I was disregarding it. So then came the stroke."[6]

Osteoporosis, a disease marked by rapid bone loss that leads to heightened fracture risk, is a significant problem among the elderly and we should be trying to prevent it now, through bone density assessments, good nutrition, exercise, and vitamin and calcium supplements. When Lucille was hit by a car, she didn't break any bones, which she credits to her calcium pills. "Not so long ago a car sideswiped me when I was on the sidewalk, and I was hit by the side mirror. The doctor was amazed that my ribs weren't broken. My diet has lots of calcium, and I think that's why. I have a very good diet generally. I eat a lot of vegetables, including spinach, and all kinds of good things from my garden. And I take my vitamins." Georgina wishes she had taken calcium sooner, and urges me to get my bone density tested. "The one thing I wish I had done at your age is start taking calcium. I should have started right after menopause. It was only when I was 60 that my doctor recommended a bone density test. I found out that I was on the verge of osteoporosis and my doctor told me I must exercise one hour per day, five days a week. That got me walking and going to fitness class. Walking has been the greatest of therapies. I walk every day. I enjoy having the discipline. No matter what I've been doing it picks me up. I go to a fitness class twice a week, I swim and I have a weekly walking group."

Several of the elders stress the importance of maintaining balance and muscle flexibility as we age, and recommend yoga and massage therapy. Lucille has peripheral neuropathy (a form of nerve damage that can affect muscle control and motor skills) and she wishes she had started massage therapy much earlier. "I'm hard on my body and my massage therapist puts my body back together every time, and she teaches me muscle-relaxation techniques. I knew that the older I get, the smarter I need to be about dealing with falls, so I went to fall-prevention class. It was great. I learned how to fall safely, and to get back up again, the right way. For one thing, I was taught not to fall on my hip. Also, I learned exercises to improve my balance, like standing on one foot." For Trudy, yoga was able to solve a medical problem that had been mystifying the doctors. "After I had two stents placed in my heart, everything was fine for several years. Then I developed staccato breathing and problems with my heart rate at night. Neither a cardiologist nor a respirologist could find anything wrong. Someone suggested I try yoga, and I figured I had nothing to lose. Thanks to yoga I've learned how to use my mind to handle my body, and I've completely overcome these rhythm problems that were so deleterious to me."

Reducing our reliance on the car is another important step to good health. When Judy turned 60, she moved to a new city and sold her car because she wanted to keep walking. "I learned to ride the bus. I knew that if I had a car I wouldn't walk." Clare chose her apartment with its central location because she could walk everywhere. Now at 90, she says, "I used to walk a lot. I would walk downtown, and then walk back. I think it was walking that kept me in shape so I was able to play tennis until I was 82."

Living Healthier and Longer—What Works, What Doesn't is a good resource for thinking proactively about our health. The authors, Carl E. Bartecchi and Robert W. Schrier, are medical doctors who wrote the book for clinicians and the public to summarize what is known about preventive health. They base their advice on documented and scientifically supported research findings, and include a section on alternative medicine.[7]

Probably the most enjoyable way to be proactive about our health is to *be happy*, because happier people tend to be healthier. Researchers assumed that happier people had healthier lifestyles. However, recent research from University College London has found that it's actually more complicated than that. It turns out that when people are happy, excited or content, they have lower levels of the stress hormone cortisol, and this is a good thing. At chronically high levels, cortisol can play havoc with our immune system, and may contribute to high blood pressure. For women, being in an upbeat mood also lowers the blood levels of proteins that are associated with widespread inflammation in the body. This inflammation seems to contribute to heart disease and cancer.[8] So, while "be happy" is not the most helpful advice, there are ways to approach this. Maybe we could use those same list-making techniques that remind us of what we should be grateful for and keep a record of what we're doing when we feel happy. This strategy supports the conclusion of Dr. Andrew Steptoe, the lead researcher on the University College London study. "We need to help people to recognize the things that make them feel good and truly satisfied with their lives so that they spend more time doing these things."[9]

If you push yourself too hard to stay young, you'll get old faster.

To get the health benefits discussed above, the elders don't recommend engaging in heroic, "pretend-you're-20-years-old" efforts. The benefits of the slow-and-steady approach to exercise are well documented. Regular low-intensity exercise improves physiologic function, cognitive function and enhances functional independence.[10] And moderate-intensity exercise for at least thirty minutes most days of the week is enough to substantially reduce cardiovascular problems.[11] As Linda says, "Don't drive yourself too hard." Sally says I should find activities that don't damage my knees, elbows or shoulders. "Don't cripple yourself. Play hard enough to have fun, but not so hard that you do damage." Taking a brisk daily walk is a better strategy than body-abusing exercise.

Dan says, "We still cross-country ski, but now do more modest tours." Georgina and her friends have also become more cautious when cross-country skiing. "We don't want any broken bones." When Henry goes for long swims in the lake his neighbours worry about him. "So now I swim with a noodle. And if I'm cross-country skiing by myself, I call the neighbours to tell them when I'm leaving and when I've returned, and I just don't push myself as hard as I used to."

Boomeritis is the label that has been given to our generation's tendency to drive ourselves too hard physically, resulting in musculoskeletal injuries.[12] In his book *Still Here: Embracing Aging, Changing, and Dying*, Ram Dass describes with unvarnished candour how, when he was well into his sixties, he pushed his body and denied his aging. He boogie-boarded with twenty-year-olds and wound up impaled on a coral reef, he tried to impress a youthful golf instructor by acting her age and ripped his rotator cuff and he nearly collapsed trying to keep up with young workers while helping a friend build his house. The story that really made me wince with empathy was what he called his "failed Superman routine" that landed him onstage in Denver with a bloody leg. "When it came time for me to take the stage," he writes, "rather than climb the steps like most sixty-three-year-olds would, my Ego, inflated from too much praise, urged me to leap from the floor to the podium. The next thing I knew I was flat on my face in front of this crowd, my leg mangled and bleeding."[13] This is one trick I'll now try to avoid.

If you deny your hearing is going, it will take you longer to hear well.

Several of the elders are using hearing aids and they warn that hearing should not be taken for granted. We should protect our hearing while we can, and, if our hearing deteriorates, we should locate the best hearing aids available as quickly as possible. We may already be experiencing hearing loss: according to the Canadian Hearing Society, 23 percent of adult Canadians report hearing loss, and 45 percent of them are between the ages of 40 and 60.[14] The loss can be so gradual we may not notice and, without realizing, we may be compensating for deteriorating hearing by using strategies such as speech reading. (This technique used to be called lip reading, but the new terminology recognizes that we do more than just read the lips—we read all the body language.)

Even if we were to admit that something is wrong with our hearing, typically we would procrastinate before seeking help. CHS finds that it usually takes seven to ten years before someone with hearing loss does anything about it. By that point, other people, such as frustrated family members, have insisted that we get our hearing tested. Experts say it's a bad strategy to wait until this point. The older we are when we get our hearing aid, the more likely it is to be an "in-the-drawer hearing aid" that gets little or no use.[15]

There are good reasons for getting a hearing aid as soon as we experience hearing loss. In general, the younger the person is, the easier it is to adapt to new devices and learn how to optimize their use. In the case of hearing aids, our adjustment is made more difficult because our experience with eyeglasses dictates our expectations. We assume that our hearing will be brought back to the equivalent of 20/20 vision, and this is not the case. Doreen is still trying to find a hearing aid that works for her. "My hearing aids don't work when there is exterior noise, and I hate being left out of the conversations." Hearing aids amplify the sound, but they don't restore hearing. Depending on the type and extent of the loss, a hearing aid may help us hear someone's voice, but we may not be able to understand distinct words. Difficulties can be amplified in certain settings, such as the dinner table, where many people are talking at once, or in places such as restaurants, where the noise level is high. And the tinny sound from the hearing aid takes getting used to. Some of these problems should improve with the advancements that continue to be made in hearing aid design.

One of the most persuasive arguments for doing something to improve poor hearing is to avoid the negative impression we risk making on people who are puzzled by our inattention or inappropriate responses. Also, hearing loss can affect independence and safety. People may sleep through deadlines because alarm clocks fail to waken them, and they may need to leave the door unlocked because they can't hear the doorbell.

The experts recommend a hearing test every two years. If you require a hearing aid, you may need two or three follow-up visits to have the device tweaked, so a grace period of at least thirty days is recommended to allow you to return the device if necessary. Once you get a hearing aid, it's recommended that you attend a hearing health class along with your significant other, to pick up communication tips and strategies, and learn what to expect. People might also benefit from assistive devices that use lights or motion to substitute for audio clues, such as an alarm clock that vibrates under the pillow.

In the meantime, what can we do to protect our hearing? Our ears never rest. They are listening all the time. The most common reason for hearing loss, after aging, is noise. The impact results from a combination of volume, proximity and duration of the sound. We can protect ourselves from loud noises by using foam inserts, and I now keep a pair in my purse for use at rock concerts or aerobic classes where they crank up the music. We should also be wary of recreational noise from Sea-Doos and Ski-Doos—not to mention those infernal leaf blowers. And after being in a noisy environment, we should give our ears a break. We shouldn't go out and cut the grass and assault them again.

There are a number of resources to help with hearing, including the website of the Canadian Hearing Society at www.chs.ca and the website of Hearing Education and Awareness for Rockers (HEAR), www.hearnet.com, a non-profit hearing information source for musicians and music lovers. *Hearing Loss: A guide to prevention and treatment* is a Harvard Health Letter that describes the causes, diagnosis and treatment of hearing loss. It includes tips to preserve the hearing we have and prevent hearing loss.[16] *Coping with Hearing Loss: Plain Talk for Adults About Losing Your Hearing,* by Susan Rezen, Ph.D., and Carl Hausman, Ph.D., focuses on the social and psychological problems that can accompany hearing loss, including how it can ruin relationships. The book includes a section for spouses, and family and friends of those with a hearing loss, as well as a section on tinnitus, a chronic ringing in the ears that afflicts many.

If you neglect your eyes, you won't like what you see.

Along with hearing loss, failing eyesight is a frustration for the elders. When we're older, if we can't see properly, we're more likely to be dependent, bedridden and dissatisfied with living.[17] Age-related macular degeneration (AMD) is the leading cause of vision loss in people over 50, and by age 75 a third of all people have it to some degree.[18] Along with age, risk factors for AMD include female gender, smoking and pale irises. (More light gets through pale eyes, which raises the risk of AMD over time.)

As with hearing, there are things we could be doing now to protect our eyesight. As it turns out, the same lifestyle choices that keep our arteries young will also reduce our chances of macular degeneration. So we need to stop smoking, control high blood pressure and diabetes, and lower cholesterol. *You Staying Young: The Owner's Manual for Extending Your Warranty*, by Michael Roizen and Mehmet Oz, has some good tips for maximizing the life of my eyeballs, including wearing dark glasses that filter out UVA and UVB rays, visiting an eye doctor every two years, sitting a safe distance from the TV screen, and taking vitamins that support eye health.

The website of the CNIB, www.cnib.ca, has an online Learning Centre with tips for eye-health care, including a primer on nutrients that protect vision, and discussions about latest research findings. Even people whose vision is too limited to read the computer screen can still participate in the online interactive discussions by using the CNIB's vocalization software. The website of Prevent Blindness America, www.preventblindness.org, a non-profit organization dedicated to saving sight, is another source of information about eye and vision health. The organization emphasizes that the effects of AMD can be mediated through early detection and treatment by an eye-care professional. Their online AMD Learning Center features a variety of resources, including tips for lowering your risk of eye disease and vision loss. There are several AMD self-assessment tools on the site, including a checklist for assessing your level of risk and an eye test using an Amsler Grid pattern. (An abnormality in the appearance of the Amsler Grid pattern may indicate macular degeneration.)

If you play an active role in your sexual health, you can stay sexually active.

The elders didn't raise the topic of sexuality, except as another example of an aging body. But healthy sexuality is part of a satisfying old age, and just because the elders didn't talk about sex doesn't mean they don't think it's important. For one thing, they might have presumed they had no sexual advice to offer to boomers who claim to have invented sex in the sixties' era of free love, and have been pushing the sexual boundaries ever since. But the most likely reason they didn't mention sex is that it's a very personal matter, and not something most of us readily discuss.

We know that old age doesn't eliminate our desire for intimacy or for sex. A recent study published in the *New England Journal of Medicine* looked at a large sample of men and women aged 57 to 85 and found that, although sexual activity declined with age, more than a quarter of the oldest group, 75 to 85 years of age, were still sexually active. The seniors who rated their health as poor were less likely to be sexually active. And, in cases where seniors lacked marital or other intimate relationships, they had reduced opportunities for sex. So the elders may have been indirectly giving us tips on sexuality through their other advice. By encouraging us to take care of our emotional circle and our physical and mental health, they could well have been saying that the sex will often take care of itself.

However, the findings from the *NEJM* study also emphasize the active role we need to play in our own sexual health. The study participants frequently mentioned sexual problems but acknowledged that they rarely discussed these problems with their physicians. The most common problems for men were erectile difficulties (achieving or maintaining an erection, anxiety about performance) and for women they were low desire, difficulty with vaginal dryness and inability to climax.[19] There are good reasons, aside from improving sexual satisfaction, for checking these things out. Untreated problems may be connected to depression or social withdrawal, and sexual problems may be a warning sign of other medical problems. We should also learn from the younger generations about the perils of unprotected sex. Over the last ten years the rate of HIV has doubled for the 50+ age group, and while the actual numbers aren't very large, the trend is significant.[20]

There are a number of resources available, both to advise us on sexual concerns of a medical nature, and to help us explore the joys of late-life sexuality. The Harvard Health Publication *Sexuality in Midlife and Beyond* discusses the physical changes that come with age that affect sexuality, and talks about medications and health conditions (including diabetes, high blood pressure, heart disease and arthritis) that can create sexual difficulties. The report includes treatments, medications and self-help techniques that can resolve common sexual problems.[21] When Joan Price was 61 years old she wrote *Better Than I Ever Expected: Straight Talk About Sex After Sixty* to help women find the pleasures in "well-seasoned sex." Price combines her own story with those of other women to share sex tips and tales, and discuss age-related sexual issues.[22] The Canadian Male Sexual Health Council is dedicated to promoting male sexual health and its website, www.cmshc.ca, includes a section on patient education.

Incontinence deserves more attention than diapers.

Along with sex, another subject that received short shrift in my discussions with the elders, and deserves more attention, is incontinence. A couple of the men admitted that a frustrating part of having an aging body is the need to pee frequently. Otherwise, the elders were silent on the subject. Incontinence, the unintended loss of urine, can have a profoundly negative effect on quality of life. The potential for humiliation can keep us housebound and contribute to depression, and if we're always rushing to the washroom we're more likely to fall and break something. Incontinence is also a leading cause of nursing home placement and, as a result, people try to hide the problem.[23] My friend describes this very situation: "According to my father, my mother suffers from 'random incontinence.' She has hidden it from everyone except my father, so I had no idea. She is so embarrassed by it that it doesn't get dealt with at all. It has been psychologically devastating for her, and has put up a barrier to her going places, entertaining, etc."

Judging by the number of TV ads for adult diapers, it looks as if becoming incontinent is just a matter of time. It's true that a significant number of older people suffer from urinary incontinence (according to Statistics Canada, 8.9 percent of men over 65, and 12 percent of women).[24] However, bladder-control problems are not necessarily a normal part of aging, and they can be treated.

Incontinence can be a symptom of another problem, so the first thing to do is rule out a medical condition. Once that's done, there are some behavioural techniques that have proven successful, including bladder training and double voiding.[25] The Harvard Medical School report "Better Bladder and Bowel Control" has some practical tips for improving bladder control. They include minimizing intake of caffeinated and carbonated drinks, decreasing or eliminating alcohol consumption, and drinking more slowly. Specific exercises, such as Kegel exercises (which many of us were encouraged to practise after childbirth), can help strengthen the muscles of the pelvic floor and shore up the muscles that control the bladder. The claim that pelvic-floor exercises could stave off incontinence is one of my bigger incentives for doing yoga. My instructor has promised me that if I practise yoga for the rest of my life, I'll never need to use adult diapers. Just in case she's right, my yoga practice is now everlasting.

Brain

To continue to act smart, you need to accept that you are not as swift.

THE ELDERS talk with frankness about the frustrations of their aging brains. They explain that older people simply can't do as much mental work as they used to, at least not with the same accuracy. As Brian says, "I notice how easily I get confused. I spend a lot of time in my head reorganizing. I'm always programming my brain to try to keep things straight." Carol feels as if her brain speed has been dialed down a few notches. "Everything is slower. My recall is slower. My speech is slower. My comprehension is slower. My granddaughter talks so fast that it doesn't get into my brain. I don't talk so much now because I can't get it out fast enough. I let others do the talking and I do a lot of listening."

What the elders have done is adopt techniques to shore up their brains. Peter finds that his mind works best when he minimizes distractions. "I try to avoid noise. I like quiet times. I don't turn on the radio or TV as soon as I come in the door. I do a lot of reflection. When I go on a long trip in the car I just think about things—what I'm going to do and say. My motto is to just keep doing it, but to slow my pace." Peter's approach is supported by neurologists who recommend that, since we lose some of our ability to filter out distracting information as we age, we should make an effort to concentrate on one key task at a time and try to reduce distractions.[1]

Several of the elders have designated a person to help them organize and stay on top of daily demands. Sylvia found that at 84 she was forgetting appointments and finding it difficult to handle all her correspondence. What is helping her keep everything straight is the assistance of a young woman who works with the non-profit organization where she volunteers. She says, "I'm not that smart, but I look for someone smarter than me to work with me in everything." Karen decided to get herself the same kind of help. She was trained as a lawyer and her work always involved writing. She still likes putting her thoughts down on paper, but at 100 years of age can no longer write legibly and can't handle a computer. Her solution was to hire a student to come to her retirement home several times a week to take dictation and handle her affairs. When I phoned Karen to arrange for an interview she explained that I would need to make an appointment through "her secretary."

The elders point out that if there are things we want to do that require intense mental concentration, we should tackle them now. For example, people with extensive libraries need to organize them while they still have the ability. An 80-year-old retired academic told me that his greatest frustration about aging has been losing his ability to lay his hands on the research documents he needs. "My files are in total disarray. If only they were in layers chronologically, then I could treat my room like an archaeological dig and shovel down to the appropriate year. But my past is lost to me now. I didn't realize I would lose the ability to sort and organize, but it's gone." Henry tried to anticipate this problem. "Once I realized I was losing my categorizing abilities, I hired someone to organize my library, but I wish I'd done it myself when I was younger. Because someone else did the organizing, I can't find things as easily as I could before. One tip that will help you as you age is to always put things in the same place. The sooner you start, the better."

One advantage we boomers will have is the increasing potential to use technological aids to keep us functioning effectively. Organizations like NECTAR (Network for Effective Collaboration Technologies through Advanced Research), www.nectar-research.net, are designing and evaluating electronic cognitive aids that will help us carry on daily activities if we develop cognitive impairments. These tools will help us remember names, faces and appointments, and find important objects such as glasses, wallets and keys, as well as help us remember procedural instructions. For any of this assistance to work, however, we first have to acknowledge we need it.

Use it or lose it.

The elders are firm believers in the "use it or lose it" philosophy when it comes to the brain, and encourage us to keep as mentally fit as possible by continuing to exercise our grey matter. They have kept their minds engaged through work, volunteer activities and hobbies. Many have taken courses and several have written books. They encourage us to follow their example.

In addition to keeping "brain fit" by staying engaged in the world, many of the elders deliberately use techniques for brain exercise. Betty is always looking for ways to give her grey matter a workout. "I deliberately don't write everything down," she says. "I try to remember things on my own. I also do exercises for my brain like Sudoku." Doreen does the same. "I do crossword puzzles and play online Scrabble. I also play bridge—it's good for the mind." The elders also found that discussion groups that focus on books or current events force them to keep thinking. Steve encourages me to memorize poetry. Research published in *Neurology*, the journal of the American Academy of Neurology, supports these strategies. The study found that people can delay the onset of dementia by doing daily cognitive exercises, whether reading, writing, completing crossword puzzles, playing board or card games, participating in group discussions or playing music. People who didn't engage their brain lost their memory three times as quickly as those who did these exercises daily.[2]

There are a variety of products that claim to strengthen the brain, each providing supportive research to back up its assertions, and each with a different focus. So, before choosing one, we'll need to figure out which mental facilities need work. For example, Brian is starting to have difficulty distinguishing words when people are speaking quickly, especially on the telephone. He says that it's not a question of volume—there is something else going on that makes it hard to tell one word from another. I have been testing out Posit Science's Brain Fitness Program, and I'm guessing that it might help Brian. The program includes exercises that focus on auditory processing—for example, distinguishing a sound that is rising in pitch from one that is falling in pitch—so it might strengthen the facility that Brian finds is weak.

There are far too many products out there to do a comprehensive listing, but a few others you might check out are available at www.mybraintrainer.com, www.brain-builder.com, and www.fitbrains.com. CogniFit products include MindFit and GoldenFit Drive for improving the driving skills of seniors, www.cognifit.com. Nintendo also offers products such as Brain Age: Train Your Brain in Minutes a Day. Most of the companies offer free trials, so if you're interested you can give these products a try.

What's good for the body is good for the brain.

Good brain functioning is also linked to our physical health, so here's where we'll get a double bang for our buck. Everything we should be doing for our body, including practising good nutrition, exercising regularly and treating medical conditions such as diabetes and high blood pressure, is equally good for the brain. Researchers from the University of Minnesota's School of Public Health followed 11,000 American participants over a fifteen-year period and found that smokers were 70 percent more likely than non-smokers to develop dementia, those with high blood pressure (hypertension) were 60 percent more likely to develop dementia than those without hypertension, and those with diabetes were twice as likely to develop dementia than those without diabetes. Another study with a similar sample size found that having even moderately high levels of cholesterol in your forties puts you at greater risk for developing dementia when you're a senior.[3]

Exercise seems to help keep our brains healthy. Researchers have found a connection between regular aerobic workouts and an increase in the number of large-diameter blood vessels in the cerebral region of the brain, as well as an increase in blood flow in the three major cerebral arteries. This is a good thing because narrowing and loss of small blood vessels likely leads to cerebral decline. Older adults who spent over three hours a week in aerobic sports for ten or more years improved their brain blood flow. Ten years sounds like a long time, and you may think you're too old to get started on this path. But it turns out that the research subjects were between the ages of 60 and 80 when they began the ten-year exercise program.[4] So maybe it's not too late to get our hearts pumping for brain fitness.

Playing is work for the brain.

If exercising seems like way too much work, we can give the brain a workout in much more playful ways. We could memorize more poetry, as Steve suggests, practise new dance steps, get back to those piano lessons we dropped as children, or take up tai chi, which my friend says has more than 240 separate movements to remember. When Fred was in his seventies, he went back to his childhood love of painting. He began by taking lessons in figure and charcoal drawing at the local art gallery, and ended up taking two years of art courses. Now at 81, he says, "I now take weekly lessons from an artist, and I do regular homework. It is something that gives me real pleasure, and I know it's good for me on so many levels." His work is getting critical approval and he has begun selling pieces both framed and as Christmas cards. "You need to develop the strengths you've got. Find the hobbies you love."

For Linda, acting is great fun as well as a great mental exercise. "Stage work is good for the brain, the memory and for focusing. The roles also teach you a great deal about the human heart, as well as [about] the people you're working with." Linda's assessment is corroborated by a research study that looked at the benefits of theatre training for seniors. The theatre participants, who were aged 60 to 86, made significant gains on measures of both cognitive and psychological well-being.[5]

Dancing plays a big part in the lives of several of the elders, and it gives their bodies and brains a workout at the same time as it brings them great happiness. The day Norah turned 65 she took her first pension cheque and bought herself dance lessons. "You need to find something that totally transforms you—and for me that's dancing. If I'm ever depressed I always dance. I remember one time in particular when I used my dancing to great effect. I was on an organized trip and they held a talent night. When it came my turn I danced the sword dance and the sailor's hornpipe. They were astonished to see me transformed from the limping lady who was always bringing up the rear." Sylvia was a dancing sensation in her youth, and, when she hit her eighties, she decided to share her love of dance by becoming a dance teacher. She ended up teaching sixty women a week to tap dance. Peter had always wanted to learn the tango so he decided he'd go for lessons to Argentina, the birthplace of the dance. "My wife and I spent two wonderful weeks in Buenos Aires taking tango lessons in the afternoon and Spanish lessons in the morning. Now we look for the chance to show off our moves."

Research findings confirm the elders' enthusiasm. Participating in the arts will benefit our brains, our bodies and our souls. The Creativity and Aging Study, conducted by George Washington University with the National Endowment of the Arts, found that community-based art programs run by professional artists for seniors have health promotion and disease prevention effects, and help them maintain their independence.[6] Those who participated in the community arts program had better health, fewer doctor visits, used fewer medications, felt less depressed, were less lonely, had higher morale and were more socially active than a control group. The study concluded that what gave the arts programs an advantage over physical exercise and many other general activities was their beauty and productivity, which fostered sustained involvement on the part of the seniors.[7]

There are several inspiring examples of these theories of aging in practice. The Zimmers is a forty-person band whose members are all over 60 years of age. One 100-year-old member is thought to be the oldest employee in Britain. It's a joy to watch them perform The Who's "My Generation" at AARP http://radioprime-time.org/specials/zimmers/. Another singing group called Young@Heart has members ranging in age from 73 to 92. They began as a lunchtime singalong at a meal site for the elderly in Northampton, Massachusetts. The group travels internationally, is recording an album and performs theatrical productions. A delightful documentary has been made about the group; the trailer is available at http://www.youtube.com/ watch?v=CjnfoFg7i7g.

The Creative Age: Awakening Human Potential in the Second Half of Life, by Gene Cohen, is an excellent resource for stimulating creativity. The book includes simple exercises and concrete suggestions to help jump-start creative energy. Another resource is *Creativity Matters: The Arts and Aging Toolkit*, which can be downloaded from the Arts and Aging website, www. artsandaging.org. The website of the Canadian Organization of Senior Artists and Performers (COSAP), www.cosap.ca, is a terrific incentive for involvement in the performing arts. One of their programs, called Jubilations, trains, nurtures and features local senior artists in professionally produced productions across Ontario. They have produced two guides to help seniors create productions in their own communities.

To stop learning is to start aging.

The elders epitomize the concept of lifelong learning. Hugh is now 90 years of age and learned to cook after he retired. "My wife did all the cooking until I left work, and then she said I should take over. I became a good cook. My best dish is cheese soufflé." When Jeanette was 54 she became a museum docent. "I was learning along with the schoolchildren. It was a gift." At 80, Stan takes courses at the community centre; his current class is about digital cameras. Louise, who is also 80, participates in a lifelong learning program run by the university. The emphasis is on peer learning, and participants write papers and present them to the class. Betsy is 75, and takes courses offered through a university continuing education program. She studied literature for three years, and read many of the classics, and took a couple of trips to France with the program. Currently she's taking a course on contemporary art, as well as lessons in watercolour painting.

For me, the most compelling argument for continuing to learn new things is the one made by Dr. Norman

Doidge, author of *The Brain That Changes Itself.* He explains that once we hit our thirties, we tend to rely on our mastery of skills in everything we do. This means we stop learning new things, and when we stop learning, the part of the brain that facilitates thinking wastes away. Eventually we lose our memory, our handwriting gets worse and we don't drive as well. This process even affects what we expect of ourselves. So what we need to do is challenge ourselves with intensive learning.[8]

A couple of the elders expressed regret about not continuing their formal learning. Sally said that if she were my age, she'd go back to school. "If you want to further your education, do it—even if you're 50. You're not too old. I wish now that I had gone back to school and finished my degree when I was your age." For those people not interested in pursuing a degree, there are countless informal learning opportunities, including programs affiliated with colleges and universities. One of the elders participates in the McGill Institute for Learning in Retirement (MILR). The program describes itself as a community of mature learners, and the emphasis is placed on "peer learning" through participation in self-directed study groups. The program encourages active participation rather than passive listening, and the groups of ten to twenty-two members are led informally by peer moderators. Members are encouraged to do research and to use the McGill Libraries. There are no educational prerequisites, no age limitations, no exams and no grades. For programs offered through other institutions, you can participate without being physically present, so even housebound people are able to enrol in an online-learning course.

The elders also take on projects as a way of motivating themselves to learn new things and to keep mentally engaged. Carol decided to pursue her interest in genealogy by tackling a family history. "I started my genealogy project and then I realized that I needed to organize all my bits and pieces—so that was my excuse for getting a computer. That forced me to learn all about the computer, too." At 92, Rosemarie gives poetry readings, and two years ago she presented a paper at a conference. "I keep mentally active by writing, researching and presenting papers." Throughout his eighties, Gordon organized dozens of gatherings to showcase literary talent, which he called his *arts and letters salons.*

Finances

Money matters, but it can't buy everything you need in Elderland.

GIVEN our society's preoccupation with money as being the secret to a successful retirement, what is striking about the elders' advice is how little of it focuses on finances. The elders have varying financial circumstances, but, regardless of income level, they seem to have what they need. Some of them describe their income as modest but adequate. Some have income from employer pension plans or retirement savings plans. Some are still working. Some, who didn't have large incomes to begin with, now find they have more money than they did when they were younger because of payments they receive from Canada Pension Plan (CPP) and Old Age Security (OAS). This is Susan's situation: "I used to have to watch more carefully, but now I could live it up—if I wanted to!"

That the elders seem to have adequate resources speaks volumes about their planning, and they suspect that many boomers are not behaving with the same kind of fiscal responsibility. "Some of the boomers don't seem to be putting aside any savings," says Dan. "You've been living in the boom years and assume that will always continue. You need to put some savings aside against your retirement." Dan's words were particularly prophetic given that he was talking to me before the 2008 recession. "You can't 'live it up' all your life and then expect to have enough put away for your eighties," Trudy says. "My husband and I were very careful to think of the future. You're going to need some money for your old age."

As the elders point out, more money means more options. "Because I have enough money, I can live on my own and hire a cleaning woman and have help with the garden," says Norah. "Also, good dental care costs money. If you can't afford a root canal, you'll need to have your tooth pulled out." Peter agrees, "You need to have a reasonable amount of retirement income to help you keep your physical and mental health. If you have failing health or resources, you might get pushed out of your home because the taxes are going up." Lucy decided to stay in her home rather than move into a retirement home because she was afraid her money would run out before she did. There were some reasonably priced government-subsidized long-term-care facilities in her city, but the waiting lists were too long. And the privately run homes she looked at were too expensive. "If I move into one of those places, it won't take long for my capital to disappear." Gordon says that having some financial resources allowed him to satisfy both his needs and his wants. "Money is very important because it gives you choices. Without some financial resources I could not have led the life I have."

A good number of seniors feel the same way as the elders. In a 2008 Canadians and Retirement survey conducted for TD Bank Financial Group, more than half of the retirees (54 percent) say that it's important to start saving early and people should make it a priority. A similar number advise pre-retirees to pay off debt before they retire. Only 43 percent of the retirees were confident that they had planned well and saved enough for retirement. Over a fifth of the retirees found that their most difficult adjustment was not being able to do the things they used to because of financial constraints.[1]

The problem is, no one can tell us how much money we'll need when we get old because it all depends. It depends on the fiscal stability of the government and its willingness and capacity to subsidize the elderly. It depends on our care needs and what it will cost to retain our independence. It depends on our own tastes and interests. Will we still love expensive wine and exotic travel right to the end? And it depends on the length of our life.

Aunt Jean is an interesting example of a wealthy life based on a limited income with riches that money can't buy. Her company pension was extremely modest, and even with the addition of government benefits, her retirement income was very low. Although the facts would place her close to the poverty level, the reality of her life as a senior was one of riches—for the simple reason that everything she wanted to buy, she could—and did. The things that really mattered to her were of the heart and were given freely. But let's look at the money first. One of her greatest joys was giving gifts to others, and by using home-shopping catalogues she was able to continue to do this until the day she left her retirement home for the hospital. All her life she managed to find just the right present for each of her family members, and she started doing the same for the retirement home staff. She also donated money to her favourite charities, right up until her death. As she aged, she spent less money, aside from these modest expenditures, because what she wanted— companionship, intellectual stimulation and fun—she received from family, friends and retirement home staff. And the things she had loved to spend money on when she was younger, like travel, no longer interested her. So, since the monthly rental at her retirement home was low and her health care costs were negligible, thanks to government subsidization, her financial demands were limited. Spending as she wished and never scrimping, even with a very low income, Aunt Jean was still able to leave an inheritance to her sisters.

Thinking about your financial future could mean a future where you won't need to think about finances.

Establishing some clear goals around their financial future was a technique that helped many of the elders. Carol had some financial struggles when she was younger, but now, at 85, is very happy with her financial position. At age 43 she left her husband and raised three children on a teacher's income. By taking evening courses, she was able to improve her credentials and increase her salary, and her pension was based on her last five years of teaching. "I have been conscious of financial matters ever since my father brought me a piggy bank offered by our local bank to encourage children to save. Things have been tight in the past, but now I'm quite comfortably settled. I can waste money, or send it off to people, or go out for lunch at the drop of a hat. The most important thing in life is to develop a financial goal and to always pursue it. You need to become financially confident."

Planning ahead also helped Brian. "When I was in my late fifties I figured out where I wanted to live and what it would cost, and realized that I wouldn't have enough to live on if I didn't make some changes. So I made some strong decisions early on. I took a new job that came with a pension and continued to work there until retirement. With this supplementary pension, my money is more than enough." William regrets not having done this. "If I were able to turn back the clock and be 50 again, I would have set myself a goal about saving money." Hugh advises me to cut up my credit cards. "Pay cash for everything. That way when you're old you'll have some money left."

Jeanette's financial preparation meant that she was able to cope when her husband developed dementia shortly after retiring. "For the first part of my marriage, my husband looked after all our financial matters. Then, when I was in my forties, I decided I wanted to handle the finances so I could become aware of what we had. I thank my lucky stars I did, because when my husband became ill, I was prepared. Make sure you understand your finances and your pension. You need to be able to manage your affairs so that you will have enough to live comfortably even if something happens to your husband. You have to be prepared. It can happen at any time."

But even the best-laid financial plans may need modifying. When Betsy was younger she sold her house and assumed the proceeds would be sufficient for a nice retirement nest egg. "I have done my best to plan financially, but if I live well into my nineties there may be a problem. I have been renting an apartment for the past nine years, but have just recently bought a condo as a better investment. I hope I will not be a burden to my children."

Sherry Cooper's book *The New Retirement* is a useful resource to help us evaluate how financially prepared we are for retirement. Cooper reminds us that our retirement nest egg will be affected by income risk (the size of our returns and the impact of inflation), contingency risk (those unexpected but necessary expenditures) and longevity risk (not knowing our lifespan). She makes the case that we boomers, in general, haven't saved enough for retirement, and she foretells the economic crisis when she urges us to make conservative estimates about future rates of return on our investments and the equity in our home. Although one can quibble with her specific recommendations regarding the optimum portfolio allocation, this next tip brooks no debate. She says the best way to reduce the strain on our nest egg is to keep working and delay drawing down our retirement savings.

The Canadian Retirement Income Calculator,[2] an online service provided by the government of Canada, is a useful exercise to estimate the ongoing income you may receive throughout your retirement from your pensions and other retirement incomes. You enter your personal information on the site, including your CPP Statement of Contributions, financial information about your employer pension (if you have one), recent RRSP statement(s) (if applicable) and statements for other savings that will provide ongoing monthly retirement income (annuities, foreign pensions, survivor pensions, etc.). The site states that the service is secure and will ensure the privacy of your personal information. It should take about thirty minutes to use the calculator.

But my favourite of all the financial resources is *Redefining Retirement: New Realities for Boomer Women*, by Margaret Hovanec and Elizabeth Shilton. The authors' goal is to help us develop a sustainable lifestyle for our retirement years, and, despite the book's title and focus, the advice is equally relevant to men. The book walks us through the construction of a Lifestyle Maintenance Budget to help us balance our income and expenditures after retirement. The authors appreciate that, for many of us, the Lifestyle Maintenance Budget won't balance in the first go-round, especially if we plan to continue our lifestyle unchanged post retirement. They walk us through some exercises of cost-cutting and income boosting, and then it's up to us to do the hard work of eliminating that gap between projected income and projected expenses. The tools include a monthly budget sheet with spending categories, and practical tips for saving money. What sets this book apart is that Hovanec is a psychologist and she understands our attachment to money and all the glittering things it can buy. She reminds us, before we make a specific purchase, to calculate the amount of life energy the item cost. Life energy is basically the time we've spent in acquiring the money that we intend to trade for the product or service. We're the only ones who can decide which trade-offs are worth it, and this exercise forces us to face the question squarely. The book's consistent message is that we have choices, and we should be making them now.

To benefit from your money, you need to draw on your emotional circle.

As we get older, we will need to identify someone we trust well enough to handle our finances if we are deemed incapable, and assign them *power of attorney for property*. As well, we need to designate someone to act as *power of attorney for personal care* to make health and personal-care decisions for us if we are incapacitated. Having been given these responsibilities for my parents, I know how critical it is to identify the right person, one who will support and empower us if our executive functions start to diminish.

Doris Marshall worked in the field of aging for four decades and in her book, *Silver Threads: Critical Reflections on Growing Old*, she tells the story of her friend Rachel. Rachel had been a successful businesswoman who fell ill during the later years of her life. Although she had the financial means to improve her situation, she lacked the capacity. Her friends knew that a paid companion would ease Rachel's anxiety and loneliness, but could not authorize the expenditure and had to turn to the trust company that was handling Rachel's affairs. The approval process required by the trust company was so lengthy that Rachel died just a few days after the companion arrived.[3]

We should also sign a living will that contains our wishes about our future health care to ensure that our intentions are honoured. This advance-care planning will provide our loved ones with guidance and will relieve them of the complete burden of decision-making. Depending on the province in which you live, living wills have different names and powers. A document called "Living Will," which explains the legal issues province by province, can be downloaded at no cost from the website of the University of Toronto Joint Centre for Bioethics.[4] This guide contains an Instruction Directive form that you can fill out to specify the kind of life-sustaining treatments you wish to be offered, as well as those you would not want, given specific health situations, including stroke, dementia, coma or terminal illness.

Leaving the party well means knowing what will happen after you've left.

Thinking through what will happen to our assets after we're gone is not an easy process, but one the elders urge us to tackle. Some of the elders hope to save sufficient resources to leave a legacy to their family and/or their community. Others are planning that their money will run out when they do. "Everyone is different," says Steve. "My wife and I developed certain habits and attitudes towards money to ensure that, at this stage of our life, we have enough for our financial freedom. We can see ourselves through to the end of our lives. I don't accept any assumption that our money is the family wealth with us as the custodians. We saw our children through education debt free, and then we gave them each $10,000. As far as I'm concerned, we have discharged our duty. But I know that, for a lot of people, leaving something to their children is very important."

The elders recommend that we work through any tough issues early on, and make sure our wishes are clearly spelled out in a will. For Marjorie, the hard question is what to do with the cottage. "The cottage is a real problem because it costs so much to maintain. The children and grandchildren love to spend time there, and we'd love to keep it in the family, but the ones who use it most are least able to afford the upkeep. We need to work this out, somehow."

Some of the elders recommend discussing our will with the beneficiaries. This was Sylvia's approach. "My husband and I sent our wills to our children and said, 'If you have a problem, now is the time to tell us.' At first our kids didn't want to look at them. But we insisted, and afterwards there were no issues. I have seen so many families torn apart by who gets what, and people stop talking to one another over a piece of furniture. I didn't want there to be any chance of this happening to my family."

Families who are caring for someone with a disability have a particular worry about what will happen after they are gone. If you are in this situation, PLAN (Planned Lifetime Advocacy Network), www.plan.ca, provides a range of products to assist you. *Safe & Secure* is a guide that sets out six steps for creating a personal future plan for people with disabilities, including: clarifying your vision, nurturing friendship, creating a home, making sound decisions, reaching financial security and achieving your plan. Worksheets are provided to lead you step by step through the planning process. *Peace of Mind* is a CD-ROM that includes personal stories, testimonials and tips, as well as worksheets.

One approach the elders suggest we consider is to donate our possessions while we are still alive. Henry owns a rural property bordering a lake and he decided to donate it to the nearby university. "The house now belongs to the university and, when they take it over, they will use it for things like lending it to visiting artists to live in, a year at a time. I have the right to stay there as long as I want and I'm not ready to leave it yet, partly because I love to swim." The elders' suggestions about donations has led me to adopt the much more modest "Creative Give-away Program" that I talked about earlier.

The Donation Planner available on the website of TriDelta Financial Partners, www.tridelta.ca, is a useful tool to help us assess how much money we can afford to give to charity every year, the tax implications of these gifts and the value of our final estate. The goal is to help us find a comfort level that balances the enjoyment of gift-giving with the need to meet our financial needs and goals.

Legacy

As you near the end, it's important to record the beginning.

THE EXEMPLARY LIVES of the elders lead me to ask myself: "What will be my legacy?" Judging by them, the answer should lie in some combination of community engagement, professional activity and family life. As another part of their legacy, many of the elders have written, or are in the process of writing, memoirs, autobiographies or family histories. They encourage us to write down memories of our life and what we know about our ancestry so that we can leave a record of our time here. And they urge us to start now, since it will become harder and harder to remember the details. Also, they warn that, once we get older, we won't be able to work on our memoirs with the same degree of energy and focus that we have now. And, after a while, we will no longer have the research skills that would help us lay our hands on the records we need.

When I asked Henry, at age 84, if there are any disadvantages to being old he said one thing in particular bothers him—he may not be able to finish his memoirs. "I'm putting it away a chapter at a time. I would like to finish it but I'm slow and undisciplined. I'm constantly being taken away from my writing because people are always asking me to do things, and I'm very weak at saying no." Norah is having a similar problem writing her memoirs. "I have kept all my diaries and I have been rereading them to prepare for writing my memoirs. But I have an awful time disciplining myself. I love gardening, and I have a big garden, so it's easy to get distracted."

Another problem for people who prefer to write in longhand is losing the ability to write legibly. As Doreen says, "I can hardly write anymore, which is very frustrating. I feel like I want to get the story together about my parents, but it's hard to get motivated. I'm glad I wrote some of my memoirs when I was younger."

The author Dave Eggers gives us the simplest and most compelling reason to write our memoirs. "You should write your story because you will someday die, and without your story on paper, most of it will be forgotten." In his introduction to *The Autobiographer's Handbook*, Eggers writes that we have a duty to write ourselves into existence. The handbook presents the details of memoir writing through round-table interviews with authors, several of whom are well known. Topics include finding your story, using research, memory triggers and interviews, shaping the story, making your story bigger than yourself, poetic licence, writer's block and blogging. Eggers says that writing one's memoir is a therapeutic process. "To delve, for a year or years, into your past, with an eye for detail and organization—to look for patterns and signals in your own life and to control its narrative . . . What could be more healing than that?"[1]

As we near the end of our life, the need to tell our story may become imperative. Mitch Albom wrote *Tuesdays with Morrie* to set down the memories and life lessons of his former professor Morrie Schwartz as Morrie lay dying of Lou Gehrig's disease. Albom used a tape recorder to capture their conversations and worried that the recording might make Morrie uncomfortable. Morrie responded, "You don't understand. I want to tell you about my life. I want to tell you before I can't tell you anymore. I *want* someone to hear my story."[2]

And neglecting your family history can bring regrets. Hugh, now 98, says that if he were able to turn back the clock and be 50 again he would spend more time understanding his past. "I ignored my father. I wish I had asked him about our forebears and what he knew of the family history. When my sister died, I lost my last chance to find out about my family's past. I can't ask any questions now, and that's a real loss." Hugh advises me, "Try to talk to your parents more than you generally do, even though it's not always easy. Don't let some little thing stand in the way. People don't spend the time needed to get the best from their family."

By preparing our story we will make it easier for others to help us if we lose our mental capacities. Dr. Ron Baecker has been working with patients at Toronto's Baycrest Centre for Geriatric Care to create multimedia biographies using photos, interviews and biographical information. Baecker finds that these biographies give patients a positive self-identity and bring them some calm and joy. They also assist family members to remember their loved ones as they once were.[3] However, producing these biographies relies on information that is much easier to pull together before the disease sets in.

If you remember your life, your life will be more memorable.

For many of us, our daily schedules are so jam-packed we have a hard time remembering what we did a few weeks ago, let alone last year. If we decide to look back and try to make sense of our life, will we ever be able to recall the decades of details? Many elders recommend we start to keep a daily journal, or at minimum, make a recording of special events. A remarkable number of them have put their stories down in trip reports, journals, even books, and one elder has recorded his memoirs on CD.

Once she turned 65, Deirdre began to keep a regular journal. "I looked forward every morning to having a self-discussion about what was concerning me. Now, I use my journal to look up dates and recapture the memory of how I felt at the time. My husband urges me to continue my writing, but now that I'm 83 I find it hard to find the energy. I'm glad I did it when I did, and I wish I'd started even earlier. You should start doing this now." Henry is writing his memoirs at age 84 and regrets not having kept a diary. "As I write my memoirs, I find that there are facts and things I would like to know that I've completely forgotten. Keeping a diary is a very helpful tool for recording your activities, and I wish I'd done it."

If keeping a diary is too onerous, the elders have less time-consuming suggestions. Steve recommends keeping a simple chronology of events—a recording of what happened when. "My wife and I have done a lot of work on our family histories and I've started a simple schedule to keep things up to date—this month we did this—so we can remember what happened." Henry suggests annotating the books we're reading. "As I read authors like Proust and Dostoevsky, and poetry to a lesser degree, I've always annotated my books with my thoughts. It has been very helpful to be able to reread my comments and remember what I thought then." Gordon took all his personal files and synthesized them into autobiographical stories that he recorded on a number of CDs. He is a natural storyteller. "I decided to use this technique because it let me tell my story in the manner in which I seem to be most at ease. These audio stories will be my bequest." Georgina has started keeping trip diaries. "Now when we do trips we write them up and add photos. It helps us recall the trip."

A number of the elders were lucky that people saved their letters. This was the case for Lucille. "I'm very fortunate. When my mother died I found that she had saved a good many of my letters. Reading them now, I am amazed. I was so busy, I just think, 'How did I do all that?' I am separating the letters that relate to my children into four envelopes so that they can each have their own record of their history." When Barbara left home to pursue education, travel and work, she promised her parents that she would send them weekly letters. She continued the tradition for years and her parents faithfully saved every letter. "I have all these letters and they are a wonderful record of my life at the time."

The tradition of keeping correspondence, our own and others', has become easier with email. And a variety of digital media is available to record and store our personal and family history. Tools such as digital cameras, techniques such as blogging, and software such as Apple's iLife can record our every thought and move, and help us turn our reminiscences, photos and music into photo books or movies. One challenge with all these media is devoting the time to storing the products in a manner that is retrievable both from the perspective of technology and information retrieval. We'll need to set up a digital filing system that will continue to make sense to us as we age. And we'll need to keep updating to the latest technology so that we don't find ourselves in a position where the original software is no longer readable, or the medium is no longer supported. Steve is in the middle of this process. "We're transferring our 35mm slides to computer, or throwing them out." Of course, none of this will be possible unless we make an effort to keep mastering these new technologies. We could follow the example of the elders by taking courses, heading for the library and hiring young tutors.

More than one brain can access your memories.

The elders encourage us to get help with our family history because it will make the job easier and more enjoyable. Norah has used both group and one-on-one support to help her write her memoirs. "My family and I have recorded various people, and we have written short bios, so I have lots of material to use. I'm well along, but I have to do it all on my own. So I decided to get some help by joining a memories group. In the group we're all women in our eighties, and we're all at different stages of writing. I'm also working with a woman I hired personally to help me. She gives workshops on memoir writing. Sharing the family history with my kids is a big responsibility. If I don't do it, these stories will be lost."

There are a variety of companies that will capture our family history in our medium of choice, whether website, video, audio, CD or print. The Association of Personal Historians, www.personalhistorians.org, lists their members in Canada. There are a number of self-publishing companies, including Trafford Publishing, www.trafford.com, and Lulu Publishing, www.lulu.com.

Some of the elders are recruiting family members to help with the task of recording family history. Some are using travel as a way to stimulate the interest of family members in their heritage. Louise will celebrate her eightieth birthday by coordinating a family visit to her hometown. "My children and grandchildren will come with me to visit the town where I grew up, and they'll hear my stories about life back then. My intention is to get my family to know something about their roots. All fifteen of us will stay together for a week, and we will have a luncheon with old friends." Georgina has been working on a family history over a twenty-year period, and was able to track down some lost relatives. "We've visited back and forth and through this process my children have really gotten interested in their heritage. That's been a great bonus."

Aunt Jean enlisted me to help record the family stories that she had learned from her parents. She was the sole repository of my maternal history, and once she reached her eighties I realized that we needed to capture her storehouse of memories while we were still able. We worked out a process whereby she would write her stories in longhand, and I would type them up for her to review and edit. Then, with her history in hand, I went to Scotland with my family to seek out the people and places she described, including our clan's ancestral home and its chief. I then combined her research and our trip report into a narrative of family history. As my aunt reached the end of her life, it gave her great pleasure to see the family's heritage taken seriously, and it relieved her greatly that the past wouldn't die with her. The process connected me with my aunt and with the maternal side of my family, and introduced my children to some fascinating personal history.

The Future

THE ELDERS have given us good advice about what we should be doing to become competent and engaged seniors, but they remind us that this will be insufficient to ensure a good future. If we wish to live well in our later years, we would need to change not just ourselves, we would need to change society. Then all elderly people would be able to lead lives of dignity—not just us. This won't happen unless we focus our attention on a myriad of broad social issues.

The first thing we need to change is our attitude towards the elderly. Christine explains what it feels like to bear the brunt of the stereotypes around old age. "While I always assumed that growing old meant that I'd have to deal with failing health, I didn't realize that ageism would be part of the broader picture. Elderly people are described in such pejorative terms, such as old farts, geezers, and so on. The world at large assumes that you have little to offer. Yet some of the bravest, most interesting and most accomplished people I know just happen to be old! I hate to see them denigrated and, all too often, ignored."

At 80 years of age, Louise agrees that ageism is widespread. "The older you get, the more you are stereotyped," she says. "It is assumed that your mind is gone. It is nice to have people stand up on the bus for you, but not if it comes with the assumption that you're not 'with it' anymore." Betsy also finds attitudes towards seniors very frustrating. "One of the things that makes me mad about getting older is that people patronize us. Some of the women in my current-affairs group are no slouches. They are not sitting around in their easy chairs. In Japan, they honour older people. Not here. Here, age is equated with an inability to function." At 90, Doreen feels a similar attitude from her family. "Be prepared for your children to think that you're not in good shape, even though you feel you're in better shape than they think. It would be better if our children didn't say anything, rather than make us feel useless or incapable."

Ignorance about the elderly is certainly one reason for the lack of respect. Other than family members, how many people do we spend time with who are over the age of 75? Earlier, Lucy said the lack of contact with younger generations is what worries her most about seniors' residences, and she urged more contact among generations.

"We need to break down these barriers. We need each other and we need every generation to be there. Our society has to understand that there is some wisdom to be learned from seniors."

Stereotypes will break down when we design ways for the elderly to be visible contributors to society. Forward-thinking communities are already looking at what needs to be done, and, in North America, California is leading the way—from necessity. People over 65 already make up over 10 percent of the state's population, and in the next twenty-five years a doubling of the senior population is forecast. Here are some examples of how Californians are approaching a rapidly aging population:

- In Contra Costa County, where 50 percent of the residents are baby boomers, a non-profit organization called Contra Costa for Every Generation launched a planning process involving 400 stakeholders (www.foreverygeneration.org). The process is called "Making Our Community Aging-Friendly," and the goal is to make their communities good places to age, where people stay healthy, live independently and lead full and productive lives.
- The California Employment Development Department has developed an employer toolkit called "Profit from the experience of a lifetime,"

which can be downloaded from its website at www.edd.ca.gov/emptoolkit.pdf. The purpose of the project is to help employers address their skilled-labour shortages by adopting age-neutral and innovative hiring, training, retention and benefit-package policies.

- Angelus Plaza, located within walking distance of downtown Los Angeles's many cultural attractions, is home to 1,300 low-income adults with an average age of 78 who pay rent geared to income. The Angelus Plaza Senior Activity Center is open to the community at large and supports independent living with an on-site health clinic, job training and volunteer placement. For more information see www.rhf.org.

- The Senior Center in Westminster runs Project S.H.U.E. (Safety, Health, Understanding and Education), an intergenerational program that pairs seniors with at-risk schoolchildren for mentoring and tutoring. Many of the seniors speak Vietnamese or Spanish and have never worked outside the home. The seniors gain employable skills and the children gain valuable life and educational support.[1]

Denmark and Sweden are the very best places to grow old, according to Canadian journalist Judy Steed, mainly because they do everything they can to encourage seniors to lead lives of proud independence. These countries provide assistance to seniors to allow them to remain in their own homes for as long as possible, and, after that, they provide supportive care facilities. Steed's investigative series *Boomer Tsunami*, published in the *Toronto Star*, effectively gives us a to-do list to prepare for Canada's aging population. Here are a few examples of our tasks: establish an effective long-term home-care system, train more geriatricians, stop overmedicating seniors, provide incentives to encourage seniors to exercise their bodies and their brains, transform the culture of nursing homes to encourage senior independence, support seniors in their own home with housekeeping and groundskeeping, combat elder abuse and provide peer counsellors to combat isolation.[2]

Lillian Zimmerman urges us to take charge of our future in *Baglady or Powerhouse?: A Roadmap for Midlife (Boomer) Women*, and she categorizes her strategies as Resenting, Resisting and Reconstructing. The actions she suggests range from the immediate and personal to the policy-based and societal, and would result in a much-improved world for both the elderly and the young. Zimmerman's suggested changes for our own behaviour include avoiding such phrases as "I'm having a senior's moment" or using senior jokes that demean ourselves and others. When it comes to global change, her dreams include maturity centres (to replace seniors centres), which include daycare (for those who are caregivers for their grandchildren) and maturity advocacy groups, "which will be nationally organized to act as a powerful lobby on behalf of matures."[3] Zimmerman is herself over 80, so she has first-hand experience with the subject, in addition to her professional credentials as an adult educator and a gerontologist.

Barbara, one of the elders, finds when she travels in the developing world her advanced years bring instant respect, especially in rural communities. "I was in a precarious position one time, where bandits were discussing kidnapping me, and they decided to let me go when I took off my scarf and they saw my white hair." She says that Canada needs to learn from other countries when it comes to treatment of the elderly, and she gives me this example. "The Chinese National Council on Aging has volunteer members who help the elderly by bringing them groceries and getting them out. People are encouraged to start volunteering from the age of 30 and each hour they donate is recorded. When they turn 60 they can start drawing down. The number of hours they contribute determines the number of hours they'll be able to use." Barbara recommends Help Age International, www.helpage.org, as a good source of information. The organization, active in seventy-five countries, has a vision of a world in which all older people can lead dignified, active, healthy and secure lives.

Peter recommends that we learn from the Aboriginal peoples, who have much to teach us about respect for the elderly. "In First Nations communities they always consult the Council of Elders. We should value the people in our society who have a lot of experience." We also have much to learn from the disabled community that has insisted on the right of its members to be full contributors to society and has made great strides in gaining respect and integration for the differently abled.

As well as learning from the disabled, we can form practical alliances with their organizations. For example, the city of Regina made more effective use of special transit vehicles by combining the needs of physically impaired seniors with those of younger impaired persons. This illustration is found in Gerald Hodge's book *The Geography of Aging: Preparing Communities for the Surge in Seniors*, discussed earlier. Hodge recommends that every community in Canada develop what he calls a "Senior-Smart" community plan to prepare for the needs of the aging population. He recommends that the plan have two underlying principles: enabling seniors' independence through supportive programs and services; and providing facilities for a continuum of care. This continuum of care would move from well elderly, to the frail elderly living at home, to the functionally impaired elderly living at home, to the functionally impaired elderly living in facilities requiring round-the-clock medical care, to the ill elderly who require intensive medical care.

Embracing Old Age

LEARNING from the elders has made me rethink my whole concept of the aging process. I now understand that strengthening my relationships with my friends and family and having the right partner will help me accept my diminishing body and brain with more humour and equanimity. The same goes for my finances. I'll need to adjust my lifestyle to my income, and that will be easier to do if I build up my emotional circle and develop some major self-awareness. When it comes to civic engagement, I need to get involved now, and when it comes to work, I should figure out how to stay in the game. The word "retirement" should be eliminated from my vocabulary since it seems to have outlived its usefulness. There are lots of things I can do to keep my body and my brain healthy, but I need to plan my workouts with a realistic assessment of my capacities. And many of the workouts could be a great deal of fun, especially the tangos, the painting and the theatrical productions. I'll be better able to navigate Elderland if I pare down, travel light and start organizing all those files. I now understand why so many of my older friends are discovering their roots, and I am earmarking some family offshoots that warrant my exploration.

If I had to sum up in one sentence what I've learned from the elders, it would be, "I must plan for old age so that I can embrace it." This will be a radical departure for me since, like so many of my generation, I've been working to stay forever young. The elders are not in denial about what life has taken away from them, but they have also come to understand what old age has given them. And they are greedy for more. There's Barbara stomping off into parts unknown using her white hair to sweet-talk bandits into releasing her. There's Marie, sashaying around her retirement home making a walker look like a high-end accessory. There's Fred selling his Christmas cards with his artwork signed with a flourish. There's Georgina building up her bones and her friend-ships with non-stop activity. There's Henry swimming with a noodle so the neighbours won't worry as much. There's Lucy making a home for young men from war-torn countries and challenging herself to keep reach-

ing out. There's Gordon and his bizarre sound amplifier walking up to total strangers and inviting them to
brunch—and being engaging enough that they accept
the invitation. There's Carol and her gang playing bridge,
having breakfasts and birthday parties and supporting
each other every inch of the way. There's Norah singing
"Old MacDonald" on the street, and Hugh laboriously
writing letters in longhand, telling politicians what he
thinks. There's Jeanette visiting her husband who has
dementia and telling him stories about the times they
stole off on hot summer nights to swim together in the
river. There's Deirdre and her husband still thrashing
it out with the help of a counsellor because they love
each other and want to make their relationship better.
There's Marjorie and her granddaughters negotiating the
favoured privilege of carving the butter rose. There's
Stan sticking with his curling even though he has to do
the modified version for people who can't bend down,
and must continually wipe his runny eyes and nose.
There's Sylvia making all those memories at her cottage,
first with children, then grandchildren, and now great-
grandchildren. There's Peter working away at a job without the status or resources of his earlier positions because
he still believes you can improve the human situation.
There's Joan downsizing to a condo on the "wrong side
of the tracks" so she can be with young people and live
in the heart of the action.

Then there's my dear aunt Jean. It was only when I saw her in the hospital after her stroke that I fully realized she was nearly 90 years old. She was paralyzed and could only communicate with eye movements and grunts. The young doctor took one look at her and said, "I can tell by that twinkle in your eyes that you love to talk and you are so frustrated that you can't speak to us." Jean acknowledged the doctor's empathy with a look of profound gratitude. I added, "What is really annoying my aunt Jean is that she can't put on her face," and she grunted with amusement at the truth of this. But even locked in, unable to eat or breathe on her own, and barely able to communicate, Jean refused to be moved to the palliative care ward to wait for the end. Instead, she nodded an agreement to the doctor to authorize a risky operation that might just prolong her life. She lost the gamble and died shortly after surgery. But right to the end she refused to fold. The house had to pull in her chips.

The elders have given me the gift of their hard-won experience. Thanks to them, I know I need to start now to ensure a successful old age, and I know what I need to do. It was a privilege to spend time with these remarkable men and women, and my only regret is that my time with them was too short. I am grateful to have been the recipient of their life lessons, and this feeling is made more poignant because several elders have passed away since I met with them. In honour of my Council of Elders, and because I believe in their wisdom, I am taking their advice to heart and implementing it as fast as I can. See you in Elderland.

Notes

1 Gerontologists label seniors by age cohort: *old* (65–74), *old-old* (75–84) and *very old* (over 85). The number of both *old-old* and *very old* has been increasing, with the number of *very old* doubling from 1991 to 2006 to over half a million people. In the decades ahead, the *old-old* and *very old* will continue to increase in both their numbers and in their share of the seniors' population. By 2031, it is estimated that 47% of seniors will be 75 or older. Gerald Hodge, *The Geography of Aging: Preparing Communities for the Surge in Seniors* (Montreal and Kingston: McGill-Queen's University Press, 2008), p. 173.

2 In 2001, nearly one-third of people over 85 required institutional care, and as many as one-half of the institutionalized *very old* suffer dementia (from Alzheimer's and Parkinson's diseases), requiring the most complex and costly care. Ibid., p. 201.

OUR EMOTIONAL CIRCLE

1 Statistics Canada, for example, found that seniors who report a strong sense of community belonging are more likely to be in good health (62%) than those who feel less connected (49%). Margot

and Laurent Martel, "Healthy living among seniors," Supplement to Health Reports, Vol. 16, Statistics Canada, Catalogue 82-003. The Harvard Study of Adult Development found that one of the most important psychosocial predictors of successful aging was having an extended family network. The other was having a high level of education. George E. Vaillant and Kenneth Mukamal, "Successful Aging," in *American Journal of Psychiatry* 2001; 158:838–47.

2   Jessica Allen, *Older People and Wellbeing*, London, England: Institute for Public Policy Research, July 2008, p. 27.

3   According to research conducted by the Rush Alzheimer's Disease Center as reported in the February 2007 issue of *Archives of General Psychiatry*.

4   Dr. Michael Evans sees daily evidence in his medical practice. He says, "If I had a prescription for loneliness my day would be a lot easier." And "Social isolation can be as powerful a risk factor as smoking." He thinks that all this talk about the health benefits of the Mediterranean diet is simply measuring the wrong variable. Michael Evans, "Social threads are tied to your well-being," *Globe and Mail*, November 27, 2007. Malcolm Gladwell discusses this theory of the Mediterranean diet in *Outliers: The Story of Success* (New York: Little, Brown and Company, 2008), p. 9. The original research was done by John G. Bruhn and Stewart Wolf in the 1970s, looking at people from the town of Roseto, in southern Italy, who emigrated to eastern Pennsylvania and retained their good health by transplanting their social structure.

5   Currently two-thirds of seniors over 75 who receive help with daily chores get it from a relative. Martin Turcotte and Grant Schellenberg, *A Portrait of Seniors in Canada*, Statistics Canada, 2006, Ministry of Industry, p. 155.

6   *The Geography of Aging*, Hodge, p. 203.

7   Turcotte and Schellenberg, *Portrait*, p. 144.

8   Ibid., p. 145.

9   Dr. Gene Cohen, *The Mature Mind: The Positive Power of the Aging Brain* (New York: Basic Books, 2005), p. 161.

10   Ibid., p. 148.

11   Stephanie Clifford, "Online, 'a Reason to Keep on Going,'" the *New York Times*, June 2, 2009.

12 As described by Daniel Goleman in *Emotional Intelligence: Why It Can Matter More Than IQ* (New York: Bantam Books, 1997).

13 Margaret Laurence, "Prospects for Peace," *Homemaker'sMagazine*, 1986.

14 Carl Jung, in Joseph Campbell (ed.), *The Portable Jung* (New York: Penguin Books, 1971), p. 14.

15 Stephen Miller, *Conversation: A History of a Declining Art* (New York: Yale University Press, 2006), p. 4.

16 Research conducted by Dr. George Vaillant for the Harvard Study of Adult Development has followed hundreds of men over seven decades of life. For purposes of the study they defined someone as having a stable marriage if they were married without divorce, separation or serious problems until age 50. George E. Vaillant and Kenneth Mukamal, "Successful Aging," in *American Journal of Psychiatry* 2001; 158:838–47. The findings of the longitudinal study are discussed in Vaillant's book *Aging Well* (Boston: Little, Brown and Company, 2002). More recent research by Hughes and Waite that looked at both men and women found that people who spent more years divorced or widowed have more chronic health conditions and mobility limitations. "Those who have married once and remained married are consistently, strongly and broadly advantaged." Mary Elizabeth Hughes and Linda J. Waite, "Marital Biography and Health at Midlife," September 2, 2008, p. 21. See http://psychology.uchicago.edu/people/faculty/cacioppo/jtcreprints/ hw09.pdf.

17 Data from the 1998 survey *Divorce in the Netherlands* (N = 2,223) was used to analyze differences in loneliness among divorced and married men and women. Divorcees who attach great importance to having a partner and people whose marriages are conflict ridden tend to have the highest levels of emotional loneliness. Pearl A. Dykstra and Tineke Fokkema, "Social and Emotional Loneliness Among Divorced and Married Men and Women: Comparing the Deficit and Cognitive Perspectives," in *Basic and Applied Social Psychology*, Vol. 29, Iss. 1, April 2007, pp. 1–12.

18 As one example of the research supporting this conclusion, the following study found that partners in happy marriages had significantly lower blood pressure compared with singles, even those with

a network of social support. See J. Holt-Lunstad *et al.*, "Is there something unique about marriage? The relative impact of marital status, relationship quality, and network social support on ambulatory blood pressure and mental health," *Annals of Behavioral Medicine* 2008; DOI: 10.1007/s12160-008-9018-y.

19   Bill Hendrick, "Bad Marriages Take Health Toll on Women," *WebMD Health News*, March 4, 2009, http://www.medicinenet.com/script/main/ art.asp?articlekey=98266.

20   Currently, 43% of all Canadian retirees are single. Augusta Dwyer, "Solo fliers buck the headwinds," *Globe and Mail*, February 25, 2009, p. E6.

21   Statistics Canada reports that immediate family members represent nearly half of all ties in the social network of those seniors aged 75 and over. Op. cit., Statistics Canada, 2006, p. 150.

22   Ibid., p. 155.

23   Ibid., p. 147.

24   Ibid., p. 146.

25   Merril Silverstein *et al.*, "Reciprocity in Parent-Child Relations Over the Adult Life Course," *Journal of Gerontology: Social Sciences* 2002 57:S3-13.

26   A University of Southern California study followed mothers and their offspring over fifteen years and found that when the mothers were in their mid-sixties to late seventies, those who got the most emotional support and practical help from their grown children had provided similar help to their own parents, as well as having formed strong emotional bonds with their children. Marilyn Elias, "Treat your children, and your parents, well," *USA Today*, http://www.usatoday.com/news/health/2007-11-19-parentscare_N.htm.

27   Simone de Beauvoir, *Old Age* (Middlesex, England: Penguin Books, 1970), p. 528.

28   Guided visualization or guided imagery is used as part of a meditation practice to invoke particular states of mind. A good primer on these techniques is found in Jon Kabat-Zinn, *Full Catastrophe Living* (New York: Bantam Dell, 2005), which is used as part of the program of the Stress Reduction Clinic at the University of Massachusetts Medical Center.

29 Ram Dass wrote *Be Here Now* in 1971 when he was known as Richard Alpert. He proposes that we imagine "these enemies" as "souls with their own suffering and ignorance." Ram Dass, *Still Here: Embracing Aging, Changing, and Dying* (New York: Riverhead Books, 2000), p. 124.

30 Elisabeth Kübler-Ross and David Kessler, *On Grief and Grieving* (New York: Scribner, 2005), p. 31.

SELF

1 Carl Jung, in Joseph Campbell (ed.), *Portable Jung* (New York: Penguin Books, 1971), p. 17.

2 "I'm going to be 50, it's about time I got to know myself."

3 In addition to psychological benefits, journaling can have physical health benefits, particularly if you are writing about traumatic events in your life. The *Journal of the American Medical Association* reported a study in which patients with either asthma or rheumatoid arthritis were asked to write about the most stressful event of their lives. They showed greater improvement in lung function or improved health status, as compared to a control group writing about emotionally neutral topics. Researchers surmise that expressive writing helps people develop a coherent narrative of their experiences, which leads them to develop a more adaptive understanding of themselves and others. One interesting finding is that expressive writing may be particularly beneficial for men. An article in *Advances in Psychiatric Treatment* reviews the research findings on this topic and includes specific suggestions for the clinical use of expressive writing. Karen A. Baikie and Kay Wilhelm, "Emotional and physical health benefits of expressive writing," in *Advances in Psychiatric Treatment*, 2005, Vol. 11, 338–46.

4 This short story, written by Anton Chekhov in 1899, is about an affair that takes place in the seaside resort of Yalta between two married people: 40-year-old Gurov and Anna, who is ten years younger. Gurov is a practised seducer, and intends the dalliance to be short-lived and pleasurable, whereas the inexperienced Anna is

ashamed of her behaviour. Despite himself, Gurov finds that in his relationship with Anna he is falling truly in love for the first time. The story ends with the couple's decision to find a solution that would let them be together without deception and secrecy.

5 Galsworthy's theme in this and other work is the damage caused by suffocating social codes and stifling class conformity, and it appears that this was familiar territory. He became a lawyer, like his father, despite the fact that he preferred writing to practising law. It was only after his father's death that he began publishing under his own name, and only then did he marry the wife of one of his cousins, with whom he'd begun an affair ten years earlier.

6 A study published in the *Canadian Medical Association Journal* found that suffering a hip or spine fracture can significantly increase the odds of an early death in people aged 50 and over. More than 23% of people who suffered a hip fracture died in the study's follow-up period, while 18% of men and nearly 16% of women with spinal fractures died. Other fractures did not seem linked to a significantly increased risk. Carly Weeks, "Spine and hip fractures linked to early death," *Globe and Mail*, August 4, 2009.

7 Reported in Carol L. McWilliam, William L. Diehl-Jones, Jeffrey Jutai and Saeed Tadrissi, "Care Delivery Approaches and Seniors' Independence," *Canadian Journal on Aging*, Vol. 19, Suppl. 1, 2000, pp. 102–24.

8 This is a faint foreshadowing of the variety of tools in development. If you are interested in what may be available when you need it, have a look at the work being done by NECTAR (Network for Effective Collaboration Technologies through Advanced Research), www.nectar-research.net.

9 Ram Dass, *Still Here: Embracing Aging, Changing, and Dying* (New York: Riverhead Books, 2000), p. 196.

10 Martin Turcotte and Grant Schellenberg, *A Portrait of Seniors in Canada*, Statistics Canada, 2006, Ministry of Industry, p. 52.

11 Research cited at the Annual Convention of the American Psychological Association found that older adults are more likely to avoid negative, stressful situations than younger adults. This is one of the reasons that emotional happiness improves with age. APA press release, August 7, 2009. http:// www.apa.org/releases/aging-21st.html.

12 Simone de Beauvoir, *Old Age* (Middlesex, England: Penguin Books, 1970), p. 542.

13 www.graypanthers.org.

14 http://www.vcn.bc.ca/ragigran.

15 In a study reported in *Journal of Personality and Social Psychology*, August 2002.

16 Val Paape, "Mindful Liberation," in *Bringing It Home*, Brenda Lea Brown (ed.) (Vancouver: Arsenal Pulp Press, 1996), p. 303.

17 Ibid., p. 305.

18 "Take control now: advice from Canadian retirees to those next in line," press release: May 12, 2008. The Canadians and Retirement survey was conducted by Angus Reid Strategies in March 2008 for the TD Bank Financial Group.

19 Richard Cohen, *Blindsided: Lifting a Life Above Illness: A Reluctant Memoir* (New York: HarperCollins, 2004), p. 225.

20 The film is available from the National Film Board of Canada at http:// www.onf-nfb.gc.ca/eng/collection/film/?id=51620.

21 The study of humour and laughter and their effects on the body is the focus of the study of gelotology. (*Gelos* is Greek for laughter.)

22 R. Morgan Griffin, "Give Your Body a Boost—With Laughter," 2006, http://women.webmd.com/guide/give-your-body-boost-with-laughter

23 Kataria's website, Laughter Yoga International, is at www.laughter yoga.org

24 P.B. Baltes and M.M. Baltes, "Savoir Vivre in Old Age," *National Forum*, Spring 1998, Vol. 78, No. 2, pp. 13–18.

25 As an indication of popular preoccupations, an email is circulating through my network reminding us that there are three things in life that, once gone, never come back: Time, Words, Opportunity.

26 Neal J. Roese and Amy Summerville, "What We Regret Most . . . and Why," University of Illinois, PSPB, Vol. 31, September 2005, 1273–85. For a fascinating discussion on finding or *not* finding happiness, including how we deal with regrets, I recommend Daniel Gilbert, *Stumbling on Happiness* (Toronto: Vintage Canada Edition, 2007).

27 A program in which nursing home residents were visited regularly by college students found that the residents improved in both cognitive

functioning and morale, as compared to a control group. See B. Reinke, D. Holmes, and N. Denney, "Influence of a 'friendly visitor' program on the cognitive functioning and morale of elderly persons," *American Journal of Cognitive Psychology*, 9, 1981, pp. 491–506.

28 John Galsworthy, *Swan Song*, Pt. II, 1928, ch. 6.

29 "Take control now: advice from Canadian retirees to those next in line," press release: May 12, 2008. The Canadians and Retirement survey was conducted by Angus Reid Strategies in March 2008 for the TD Bank Financial Group.

30 Dr. Gene Cohen, *The Mature Mind: The Positive Power of the Aging Brain* (New York: Basic Books, 2005), p. 144.

31 The study conducted by Sandra Cusack and Wendy Thompson linked the following seven mental fitness practices to healthy aging: setting personal goals, power thinking, creativity, learning and memory, speaking your mind, positive mental attitude and willingness to risk. Sandra Cusack and Wendy Thompson, *Mental Fitness for Life: 7 Steps to Healthy Aging* (Toronto: Key Porter Books, 2005).

32 Statistics Canada, 2006, p. 211. Research from the United Kingdom has confirmed this link between emotional well-being and religious beliefs in older people, and some of the benefits may well spring as much from the value of belonging to a group as the belief system per se. Researchers found that religious beliefs provide older people with a sense of purpose, and offer participation in a supportive social network. Actively participating in religious events can bring even greater benefits. Jessica Allen, *Older People and Wellbeing* (London, England: Institute for Public Policy Research, July 2008), p. 36.

33 For example, a controlled experiment reported in the *Journal of Environmental Psychology* involved 112 young adults who carried out stressful activities. "[S]itting in a room with tree views promoted more rapid decline in diastolic blood pressure than sitting in a viewless room. Subsequently walking in a nature reserve initially fostered blood pressure change that indicated greater stress reduction than afforded by walking in urban surroundings" (http://aliveltd.org/rspace/nature.html). The Restorative Spaces website http://aliveltd.org/rspace/index.html talks about a variety of techniques to incorporate in a restorative practice and emphasizes the impor-

tance of taking time for self-care. The website grew out of a project to provide hospital nurses with a virtual lounge where they could go during the workday to engage in some self-care that went beyond just putting their feet up.

34 Robert A. Emmons and Michael E. McCullough, "Highlights from the Research Project on Gratitude and Thankfulness: Dimensions and Perspectives of Gratitude." See http://psychology.ucdavis.edu/labs/emmons.

35 Mary Jo Leddy, *Radical Gratitude* (Maryknoll, New York: Orbis Books, 2002), p. 142.

36 Margaret Visser, *The Gift of Thanks* (Toronto: HarperCollins, 2008), p. 385.

37 S.J. Eggers and B.H. Hensley, "Empowering spirituality and generativity through intergenerational connections," *Journal of Religion, Spirituality and Aging*, 2005, 17 (1/2), 87–108.

38 *Expression*, Vol. 13, No. 3, National Advisory Council on Aging.

39 Norman Doidge, "The Brain That Changes Itself." Presentation at Holy Blossom Temple, Toronto, May 9, 2007.

40 Norman A.S. Farb *et al.*, "Attending to the present: mindfulness meditation reveals distinct neural modes of self-reference," in *Social Cognitive and Affective Neuroscience* 2007 2(4):313–322, http://scan.oxfordjournals.org/archive/.

41 For an excellent overview on how this research complements other findings in the area, see Daniel J. Siegel, "Mindfulness training and neural integration: differentiation of distinct streams of awareness and the cultivation of well-being," *SCAN* (2007) 2, 259–263.

CIVIC ENGAGEMENT

1 Vaillant builds on the work of Erik Erickson, the psychoanalyst who developed eight stages of development, in George E. Vaillant, *Aging Well* (Boston: Little, Brown and Company, 2002), p. 48.

2 Dr. Gene Cohen, *The Mature Mind: The Positive Power of the Aging Brain* (New York: Basic Books, 2005), p. 151.

3 The study looked at people aged 60–86. L. Fried *et al.*, "A social model for health promotion for an aging population: Initial evidence

on the Experience Corps model," *Journal of Urban Health* (1), 64–78, www. civicventures.org/experience_corps.cfm.

4 The book can be ordered from www.volunteervancouver.ca.

5 The Urban Institute analyzed data from the U.S. Health and Retirement Study to examine formal volunteer activities as individuals move from work to retirement. Sheila R. Zedlewski, "Will Retiring Boomers Form a New Army of Volunteers?," *Perspectives on Productive Aging*, December 2007, Urban Institute, Washington, D.C., www.urban.org.

6 About two-thirds of Canadians who don't volunteer cite lack of time as their reason. "Business Support for Employee Volunteering in Canada: Results of a National Survey," Imagine Canada, 2006.

7 Ibid., p. 44. The Canadian Corporate Council on Volunteering promotes the benefits of employer-supported volunteerism and seems to be making a persuasive case. Since the formation of the council in 2005, there has been steady growth in the number of paid hours employees are given for volunteering. In 2005, employees in fifteen companies contributed 150,000 volunteer hours. In 2007, twenty-three companies donated more than 475,000 hours. For more information see volunteer.ca. SaskTel and McGill University Health Centre provide examples of workplace-supported volunteerism in action. In Regina, younger workers at SaskTel receive company support for Next Gen, a project that provides communities in Africa with donated equipment, including medical and school supplies, clothing and bicycles. The employer pays project costs, including travel expenses for the SaskTel employees who go to Africa to unload and distribute the donations. The employees' flexible work schedules allow them time for their volunteer commitment. (Source: "SaskTel dials in to community involvement," Danielle Harder, *Canadian HR Reporter*, January 26, 2009.) The McGill University Health Centre gives unpaid humanitarian leave to its employees, which has allowed them to assist in disasters such as the 2004 tsunami and Hurricane Katrina. The centre's associate director of human resources says, "They know they still have their job here and come back happier and with an additional experience," in Danielle Harder, "Hospital finds cure for retention: Time off," *Canadian HR Reporter*, January 12, 2009.

8 "Caring Canadians, Involved Canadians: Highlights from the 2004 Canada Survey of Giving, Volunteering and Participating," Statistics Canada, Minister of Industry, 2006, p. 34.

WORK

1 *Lost Horizon* (1933) is a novel by British author James Hilton (made into a movie of the same name in 1937) about the fictional utopia of Shangri-La where people aged so slowly they were almost immortal, as long as they never left their utopia. Once they did, age caught up to them immediately. See www.losthorizon.org.

2 Tu Thanh Ha and Virginia Galt, "More Canadians delaying retirement, study finds," *Globe and Mail*, September 10, 2008.

3 RBC poll conducted by Ipsos Reid, November 2007, www.rbc.com/newsroom/20080415survey.html.

4 RBC poll conducted by Ipsos Reid, November 2007, www.rbc.com/newsroom/20080415survey.html. Currently, 85% of people aged 65 or over who work part-time are doing so because of personal preference. Ibid., Statistics Canada, 2006, p. 118.

5 According to a 2007 survey, two-thirds of workers when they hit retirement age would prefer to stay with their current employer and change jobs, rather than work for another company. RBC poll, ibid.

6 Tamara Erickson, *Retire Retirement* (Boston: Harvard Business Press, 2008) includes a useful chapter on renegotiating the deal with your employer.

7 Simone de Beauvoir, *Old Age* (Middlesex, England: Penguin Books, 1970), p. 261.

8 "Slap on these shoes for a whole new way of walking," *Globe and Mail*, November 8, 2008.

9 Of the 109 mid- to large-sized Canadian organizations included in the survey, only 6% focus on retaining mature workers and 11% actively try to attract or recruit them. However, over three-quarters of the employers think that the aging of the workforce will be an important or critical issue in the next three to five years. "Harnessing the Power: Recruiting, Engaging and Retaining Mature Workers," Conference Board of Canada, 2008.

10 See www.workplaceinstitute.org.

11 The program is sponsored through the MetLife Foundation and Civic Ventures (www.civicventures.org). The career changes are from the 2007 winners of the Breakthrough Award. More examples of career changes are available at www.2young2retire.com, a website run by George Kinder, a financial planner, author and seminar leader.

12 Martin Turcotte and Grant Schellenberg, *A Portrait of Seniors in Canada*, Statistics Canada, 2006, Ministry of Industry, p. 119.

13 Sara Davidson, *Leap!: What Will We Do with the Rest of Our Lives?* (New York: Ballantine Books, 2008), p. 8.

14 Ibid., p. 137.

15 Diane K. Osbon (ed.), *Reflections on the Art of Living: A Joseph Campbell Companion* (New York: HarperCollins, 1991), p. 181.

16 Michael Gates Gill, *How Starbucks Saved My Life: A Son of Privilege Learns to Live Like Everyone Else* (New York: Gotham Books, 2007), p. 212.

HOME

1 RBC Special Report, Toronto, March 18, 2008, based on an RBC poll conducted by Ipsos Reid, January 2008, www.rbc.com/newsroom/20080318 ownership.html.

2 *Where* is ranked at the very top along with *What*, figuring out our career, and *Who*, picking our life partner. Since *Where* has such an influence on *What* and *Who*, Florida argues that it may be the most important question of all.

3 Both Location Scout (www.aarpmagazine.org) and Find Your Best Place (www.bestplaces.net) ask you to rate the importance of such factors as climate, housing options, employment opportunities, cost of living, availability of arts, culture and recreation, as well as access to transportation, health services, continuing care and educational opportunities. Your responses are used to identify cities in the United States that most closely match your preferences. Although locations in Canada aren't included, going through the thought process is a useful exercise.

4 Gerald Hodge, *The Geography of Aging: Preparing Communities for the Surge in Seniors* (Montreal and Kingston: McGill-Queen's University Press, 2008), p. 189.

5 http://www.phac-aspc.gc.ca/seniors-aines/pubs/safelive/.

6 Adriana Barton, "Oh Dad, you shouldn't have," *Globe and Mail*, October 9, 2007.

7 Duane Elgin, *Voluntary Simplicity* (New York: Quill, 1993), p. 148.

8 Beth Powning, *The Hatbox Letters* (Toronto: Vintage Canada, 2005), p. 347.

BODY

1 "Advancing the Inclusion of People with Disabilities," Government of Canada, 2005, p. 3.

2 Gerald Hodge, *The Geography of Aging: Preparing Communities for the Surge in Seniors* (Montreal and Kingston: McGill-Queen's University Press, 2008), p. 201.

3 Hodge, p. 12.

4 Christian J. Lalive d'Epinay and Jean-François Bickel, "Do 'Young-Old' Exercisers Feel Better Than Sedentary Persons? A Cohort Study in Switzerland," *Canadian Journal on Aging* 22(2):155–65.

5 A team including researchers from the Buck Institute for Age Research found that before exercise training a sample of older adults were 59% weaker than a group of younger people, but after twice-weekly resistance training for six months their strength was only 38% lower. The younger people still had a greater capacity to lift the weights, but after six months the older people had a marked increase in their ability to carry out the exercise. http://www.plosone.org/article/fetchArticle.action?articleURI=info%3Adoi%2F10.1371%2Fjournal.pone.0000465.

6 Ram Dass, *Still Here: Embracing Aging, Changing, and Dying* (New York: Riverhead Books, 2000), p. 186.

7 The book is available for download, free of charge, at www.healthierlongerlife.org.

8 "Neuroendocrine and inflammatory factors associated with positive affect in healthy men and women: the Whitehall II study."

American Journal Epidemiology 2008 January 1;167(1): 96–102. Epub 2007, Oct 4.

9 Amy Norton, "Happiness may be good for your health," *Globe and Mail*, January 4, 2008.

10 Carol L. McWilliam, William L. Diehl-Jones, Jeffrey Jutai and Saeed Tadrissi, "Care Delivery Approaches and Seniors' Independence," *Canadian Journal on Aging*, Vol. 19, Suppl. 1, 2000, 102–24.

11 JoAnn E. Manson *et al.*, "Walking compared with vigorous exercise for the prevention of cardiovascular events in women," *New England Journal of Medicine*. Boston: September 5, 2002, Vol. 347, Iss. 10; p. 716. Also see Dakshana Bascaramurty, "Even 30 minutes a week of walking can extend life," *Globe and Mail*, August 4, 2009.

12 Andrew Wister, *Baby Boomer Health Dynamics* (Toronto: University of Toronto Press, 2005), p. 180.

13 Ram Dass, *Still Here*, p. 44.

14 *Deaf, Deafened and Hard of Hearing People: A Guide for Service Providers and Businesses*, Canadian Hearing Society, p. 15.

15 Interview with Susan Main, Vice President, Fundraising and Strategic Communications, Canadian Hearing Society, June 12, 2007.

16 http://www.health.harvard.edu/special_health_reports/Hearing_Loss.htm?utm_source=HEALTHbeat&utm_medium=emai&utm_campaign=101408. Prepared by the editors of the Harvard Health Letter, with David Murray Vernick and Rachael Rush, 41 pages (updated: 2008).

17 The Berlin Aging study found that, in addition to poor vision, the other predictive factors of poor aging are trouble walking, age per se, depression and dementia, as cited in George E. Vaillant and Kenneth Mukamal, "Successful Aging," in *American Journal of Psychiatry* 2001; 158:838–47.

18 A 2007 study commissioned for the National Coalition for Vision Health determined that an estimated one million Canadians have some form of age-related macular degeneration (AMD). The number is expected to more than double by 2031. More than one in eleven Canadians over age 65 and more than one in eight over age 75 experience severe vision loss that cannot be corrected with standard eyeglasses. See www.visionhealth.ca.

19 Stacy Tessler Lindau *et al.*, "A Study of Sexuality and Health among Older Adults in the United States," *New England Journal of Medicine* 2007 August 23:357(8):762–74.

20 *The Current*, CBC Radio, January 30, 2009.

21 https://www.health.harvard.edu/special_health_reports/sexuality_in_midli fe_and_beyond.

22 See www.joanprice.com/BetterThanExpected.htm.

23 "Taming Incontinence," *Healthbeat*, March 10, 2009. Reprinted from "Better Bladder and Bowel Control," a Special Health Report from Harvard Medical School, 2009.

24 The prevalence of chronic conditions, populations aged 65 or older, Canada, 2003, from Heather Gilmour and Jungwee Park, "Dependency, chronic conditions and pain in seniors," Supplement to Health Reports, Vol. 16, Statistics Canada, Catalogue 82-003.

25 See HealthiNation, http://healthination.com.

BRAIN

1 See W. Dale Stevens *et al.* "A Neural Mechanism Underlying Memory Failure in Older Adults," in the *Journal of Neuroscience*, 2008 28:12820–24.

2 C.B. Hall *et al.*, "Cognitive activities delay onset of memory decline in persons who develop dementia," *Neurology* 2009;73:356–61.

3 Andre Picard, "Midlife heart problems can lead to dementia," *Globe and Mail*, August 5, 2009.

4 Martha Kerr, "Exercise improves brain blood flow in older adults," December 2, 2008, uk.reuters.com.

5 H. Noice, T. Noice and G. Staines, "A Short-Term Intervention to Enhance Cognitive and Affective Functioning in Older Adults," *Journal of Aging and Health*, Vol. 16, No. 4, 562–85 (2004).

6 "The Creativity and Aging Study: The Impact of Professionally Conducted Cultural Programs on Older Adults," Final Report, April 30, 2006. The 2006 study had 300 participants ranging in age from 65 to 103 at sites in three American cities. It was the first of its kind to use an experimental design and a control group, and recorded strikingly positive results for those involved in intensive cultural programs.

7 Dr. Gene Cohen was part of the research team and explains the findings in his book *The Mature Mind: The Positive Power of the Aging Brain* (New York: Basic Books, 2005). He attributes these results to three key factors: the activities gave the participants a sense of mastery and control, the structured arts activities fostered social engagement and art, by its nature, is engaging, and therefore the activity is easier to sustain.

8 Presentation at Holy Blossom Temple, Toronto, May 9, 2007.

FINANCES

1 "Take control now: advice from Canadian retirees to those next in line," press release: May 12, 2008. The Canadians and Retirement survey was conducted by Angus Reid Strategies in March 2008 for the TD Bank Financial Group.

2 http://www1.servicecanada.gc.ca/en/isp/common/cricinfo.shtml.

3 Doris Marshall, *Silver Threads: Critical Reflections on Growing Old* (Toronto: Between the Lines, 1987).

4 See http://www.jointcentreforbioethics.ca/tools/livingwill.shtml.

LEGACY

1 Dave Eggers, "Introduction," in Jennifer Traig (ed.), *The Autobiographer's Handbook* (New York: Holt Paperbacks, 2008), p. 8.

2 Mitch Albom, *Tuesdays with Morrie* (New York: Anchor Books, 2006), p. 63.

3 Ronald M. Baecker, "Supporting Enhanced Cognition and Stemming Cognitive Decline," online presentation at the website of the Knowledge Media Design Institute, University of Toronto, March 12, 2009.

THE FUTURE

1 See http://www.ci.westminster.ca.us/depts/cs/senior/shue.asp.
2 Judy Steed, *Boomer Tsunami*, is available for download from the Atkinson Foundation website at www.atkinsonfoundation.ca.
3 Lillian Zimmerman, *Baglady or Powerhouse?: A Roadmap for Midlife (Boomer) Women* (Calgary: Detselig, 2009), p. 299.